| 8 Questions Jesus Asked |

8 Questions Jesus Asked

Discipleship for Leaders

Daniel M. Cash and William H. Griffith

FOREWORD BY SOOZI WHITTEN FORD

JUDSON PRESS
PUBLISHERS SINCE 1824
VALLEY FORGE, PA

8 Questions Jesus Asked: Discipleship for Leaders
© 2017 by Judson Press, Valley Forge, PA 19482-0851
All rights reserved.

No part of this publication may be reproduced, stored in a retrieval system, or transmitted in any form or by any means, electronic, mechanical, photo-copying, recording, or otherwise, without the prior permission of the copy-right owner, except for brief quotations included in a review of the book.

Judson Press has made every effort to trace the ownership of all quotes. In the event of a question arising from the use of a quote, we regret any error made and will be pleased to make the necessary correction in future print-ings and editions of this book.

Unless otherwise indicated, Bible quotations are from the New Revised Standard Version Bible, copyright © 1989, Division of Christian Education of the National Council of the Churches of Christ in the United States of America. Used by permission. All rights reserved.

Interior design by Crystal Devine.
Cover design by Wendy Ronga, Hampton Design Group.

Library of Congress Cataloging-in-Publication data

Names: Cash, Daniel, author. | Griffith, William H., author.
Title: 8 questions Jesus asked : discipleship for leaders / Daniel Cash and
    William Griffith.
Other titles: Eight questions Jesus asked
Description: Valley Forge, PA : Judson Press, 2017.
Identifiers: LCCN 2016031975 (print) | LCCN 2016034866 (ebook) |
ISBN
    9780817017781 (pbk. : alk. paper) | ISBN 9780817081683 (e-book)
Subjects: LCSH: Christian life. | Christian leadership--Study and teaching.
Classification: LCC BV4501.3 .C4135 2017 (print) | LCC BV4501.3
(ebook) | DDC
    253--dc23
LC record available at https://lccn.loc.gov/2016031975

Printed in the U.S.A.

First printing, 2017.

Contents

Foreword

At the root of any discovery, good questions have been asked.

Both educators and scientists know that the process of questioning is fundamental to any research endeavor. Basic questions about facts and techniques lead a learner or scholar to new inquiries, posed in original and unique ways. Sometimes complicated and innovative breakthroughs have been made because good, and often simple, questions have been asked: "What would it look like if we ...?" "Can we consider...?" "Where can we go if...?" Not all of us will be able to engage in research and discovery that results in scientific breakthrough, but no matter what our vocation may be, engaging questions and the journeys in which they lead us may unlock new places of personal discovery and innovation.

8 Questions begins with a simple reminder that "quest" is at the root of the word question and that "good questions, like their root word, always invite discovery." Joining the quest for discovery leads one to unexpected vistas, and new places of personal understanding and transformation. For those who would lead well in churches today, receptivity to this process of quest-discovery-transformation is almost a required orientation. These turbulent days of discontinuous change necessitate that a leader's toolkit be open, making space not just for additional "tools" but for the learnings and experiences that will come from engaging the process of forming and asking the right kinds of questions.

Jesus asked the right kinds of questions, and they have the power to transform our lives today. As those questions are raised and the Gospel narratives unfold in *8 Questions Jesus Asked*, readers are invited to encounter each question within its ancient cultural setting and to ponder what is happening to the other characters in the story. Every chapter focuses on a question raised by Jesus as he encountered the situation before him and as he sought to provide deeper understanding among all who were present. Each chapter proceeds to offer practical insights for life application as well as further scriptural exploration, concluding with questions for group discussion and personal reflection. An appendix provides additional resources for individual and group reflection on the themes of leadership and discipleship.

One of the strengths of this volume is the sections entitled "Implications for Life and Leadership" in which the authors delve into potential applications of the context and the question Jesus asked. Calling upon their own experiences in pastoral ministry and leadership coaching, the authors investigate concepts such as emotional intelligence, servant leadership, commitment, and change theory (technical vs. adaptive) in light of the reader's own experience with leadership and always in response to Jesus' questions. Church leaders will find these sections to be a valuable resource as they ponder navigating various ministry settings with both grace and skill.

Dan Cash and Bill Griffith have combined pastoral experience exceeding 75 years. They are both students of Scripture and keen observers of life, often pondering the rich interplay that emerges between the Word and the world. I have personally benefited from individual conversation and group interaction with each author, and I often walk away challenged, not just by the content of the discussion but by the questions that form in my mind because of the encounter.

8 Questions Jesus Asked will be a transformative guide for those who choose to join the journey by exploring the questions contained within. Some readers will want to read each chapter thoughtfully and reflect individually on the provided questions. Such learners may find the use of a personal journal to be useful in further exploring their responses and reflections. For those who are able, reading each chapter with a group and participating together in discussion and reflection has the potential to yield additional insights for personal discipleship. Life groups, leadership or discipleship groups, or any similar configuration of adult learners will find the content of each chapter, along with the format in which it is presented, to be a helpful catalyst for individual growth and the development of community.

May this powerful resource resonate with your soul, and may you be encouraged and challenged as you grow more fully as a disciple and leader.

SOOZI WHITTEN FORD
Executive Minister
American Baptist Churches of Indiana & Kentucky

Some leaders believe you must have all the answers; a wise leader knows when to ask the right question.

Introduction

This is a book about questions—specifically, questions that Jesus asked. Any perceptive reader of the Gospels will observe that Jesus asked a lot of questions. Some of them were quite direct. Others were asked to redirect. Most all of them seem to have had purpose. In other words, Jesus' questions were not just things of small talk or polite conversation; they were questions asked and used with intention.

As we study Jesus' questions, we find that they were often leadership questions. Jesus used questions to guide, develop, move, and lead others. We find him doing this consistently with his disciples, as the eight questions we explore in this book indicate. But we also find him engaging others, including those outside his circle of followers—both those who are curious and those who are opposed—with questions as well. Thus, in addition to being leadership questions, Jesus' questions often were asked with the intent to promote spiritual growth and faith formation.

In the chapters and pages that follow, we are going to explore eight questions Jesus asked. The narrative of each chapter will provide readers with information on background and context, as well as some insight into the "why" and "what" of that particular question and its use. At the close of each chapter you will find questions to use with a study or leadership group in a church or ministry setting that will further engage participants in thinking about that chapter's particular question, and their own follow-up questions about faith formation and leadership today.

1

Our dual focus may raise a question for you at the onset of the book: "Is this a book about discipleship or leadership?" The answer is yes. We believe that Jesus consistently addresses both of these topics and endeavors through the questions he asks. He invites both personal spiritual growth and leadership development in his disciples and others, including us, through his consistent use of questions.

Within congregations and ministry settings today there is a deep need for skilled leaders who are also persons of deep faith, and who see their faith formation as an ongoing process. Our hope is that this resource will encourage a deepening and development of both disciples and leaders.

Before we move forward with the eight questions, allow us to set the stage with a few more thoughts on why Jesus used questions, and how this same approach can be vital to our faith and leadership yet today.

A QUEST

When you look at the word *question*, it's easy to locate its root—the word *quest*. What is a quest? To be on a quest is to be about discovery. A quest is literally a journey of discovery. That pioneer or adventuresome spirit that resides within many of us is the fuel for a quest. Whether we set out to discover a new hobby, the cure for a disease, or information related to planning a successful family vacation, quests engage us and change us throughout our lives.

The same might be said of a good question. Like a quest, a question helps us discover. It unlocks imagination and releases us from the paralysis or stagnation of not knowing what to do next. Questions, like a quest, move us to discover something we've not known or experienced.

Consider some of the questions we find in Scripture. In chapter 3 of Genesis, after the first humans have yielded to temptation, we find God walking in the garden in search of Adam and Eve. Do you remember the questions that follow?

God asked two questions: "Where are you?" (v. 9) and "Who told you that you are naked?" (v. 11).

We submit that there was the intent of discovery behind these questions. But the questions were not so much for God's discovery as for Adam and Eve's. In other words, these questions were asked more for the purpose of *formation* than for *information*. God knew exactly where they were and why they were aware of their nakedness. God asked the questions to help them grapple with their own situation.

Similarly, in 1 Kings 19, the prophet Elijah is hiding out in a cave after a confrontation with the prophets of Baal and a fearful flight from Queen Jezebel. God's question to Elijah in verse 9 is "What are you doing here?"

The obvious and most literal answer is "I'm hiding in a cave." But the question has a depth and weight to it that invites reflection beyond the obvious. For one thing, the idiom "What are you doing?" is usually expressing the idea of "why" more than "what." So, even in everyday encounters, someone who asks, "What are you doing?" isn't really asking about the action itself but about the motive or reasoning behind the action. But when the one asking the question is God, what more may be implied in that question? Perhaps the question is partly geographic ("What are you doing *here*?"), or maybe it is contextual ("In light of all that you've just witnessed and been part of, why are you *hiding*?"). In God's question of Elijah we see how a leader is being further shaped and challenged.

Good questions, like their root word *quest*, always invite deeper discovery.

TYPES OF QUESTIONS

As our study will show, questions come in many types, and each might lead to unexpected discovery. For example, consider the story of young Billy. He came to his mother one day with the question "Where did I come from?" His mother was somewhat taken aback, but having known this day would come, she concluded it was time to tell her son the truth about the "birds and the bees"—the facts of life. Billy listened intently and then responded, "That's very interesting, Mom, but what I want to know is where did I come from— like, Tommy came from Buffalo and Ronny came from New Jersey." Mom would have been wise to first ask a question of clarification!

Staying with the theme of childhood, we note that the first questions we encounter from Jesus occur in Luke 2. Jesus has accompanied his parents on a pilgrimage to Jerusalem for the Passover Feast. He is twelve years old. A day into their return trip home, Mary and Joseph realize that Jesus is not to be found among their travel party. Many parents have had this experience of leaving a child behind somewhere, but few of us for this duration. It says in Luke 2:46 it took a total of three days for them to locate Jesus. When they did, they found him in the temple courts. What was he doing? He was asking questions, of course (v. 46).

When his parents, in their relief and exasperation, confront him, Jesus has a question for them: "Why were you searching for me? Didn't you know I had to be in my Father's house?" (v. 49).

We could read Jesus' questions with different tones, from surprise to disappointment. But in this case it appears that he was not shaming his parents, but rather reminding them of a truth regarding his identity that justified his actions. Jesus was in the temple asking questions, embarking on a personal quest to discern his heavenly Father's will. When found, Jesus used questions to help his parents discover (again) his purpose and identity as God's Son.

QUESTIONS AS A MEANS OF TEACHING

The questions we find the adult Jesus asking people, including his disciples, are consistent with a rabbinical means of teaching. Instead of lecturing, rabbis often asked questions. These questions were used to engage the disciple in the learning process and begin a dialog between teacher and students. A rabbi would begin the discourse with a question, expecting a response in the form of another question. The students' questions would then reveal something of their understanding, allowing the rabbi to then form yet another question to propel them into the Scriptures or teachings of faith.

This model is consistent with another Jewish approach to Scripture through the practice of *midrash*.[1] *Midrash*, the ancient rabbinic commentary attached to the Hebrew Scriptures, comes to Scripture with patience, humility, and respect, asking questions of the text in a formative manner. The posture of openness and curiosity allows for many possibilities and levels of faith-filled meaning. Through questions, the text, like a rabbi, can begin to read the life of the disciple and bring formation accordingly.

A good example of this dynamic in action with Jesus is found in Matthew 12:10-11. A man whose hand is withered comes to Jesus. Jesus is asked (by an opponent beginning a discourse with a rabbi), "Is it lawful to heal on the Sabbath?" He responds, "If any of you has a sheep and it falls into a pit on the Sabbath, will you not take hold of it and lift it out?" We can imagine a thoughtful pause from Jesus after this question before he goes on to say, "How much more valuable is a man than a sheep!" Question asked. Point made.

It may be that you can remember a teacher or two who employed a similar technique with questions in his or her instruction. Such a teacher may have even turned a student's question back around to the class, saying, "What do you think?" This use of question is not to make up for the teacher's lack of knowledge; rather, it reflects the teacher's desire that the students own the answer and information for themselves. Isn't this what we want for those we nurture and lead in the faith?

QUESTIONS AS A MEANS OF LEADING

We contend that you can apply the use of questions to leadership as well. Those who lead in churches today know that congregations are in the midst of a tremendous season of change. We are facing challenges of what is called *discontinuous change*. In other words, we often have no prior experience or predictable patterns to draw from when facing the challenges of ministry in today's contexts. The prototype "leader as expert" with all the answers no longer applies because the questions keep changing and we haven't found the answers yet. Today's ministry challenges—from the field of stewardship, to worship, to faith formation—require adaptation in leadership. Adaptive and collaborative leaders will realize the importance of asking questions, both of themselves and those they lead in these circumstances. Doing so will help unleash the creativity of the group, and new approaches will surface to the ever new adaptive challenges.

Learning how to ask the most helpful questions will also be important in this adaptive work of leading. One discipline that speaks to this and relies on questions is the field of leadership coaching. Coaching is simply a process of guiding a person or group from where they are toward where they want to be.[2] Coaching is founded on the belief that the potential, the creativity, and the answers reside within the persons being coached. It's the belief that through the employment of good, powerful questions—such as the types Jesus asked—that potential, that creativity, and those answers can be harnessed to unlock a leader or group from what was previously considered a stuck situation into healthy, helpful forward movement.

Phrasing or forming the right type of question is critical when it comes to using questions for the deepening work of faith formation or for the shaping work of leadership development. Coaching depends on the utilization of open, powerful questions, not closed or leading questions.

Closed questions invite a one-word answer. It is often a yes-or-no response. For example, "Did you go to the gym today?" or "Are you feeling better?"

Similarly, **leading questions** guide a person to a desired response. A question such as "You don't want to do that, do you?" does not invite the thoughtful reflection, but instead suggests a predetermined answer.

Open and **powerful questions**, however, *will* promote thoughtful responses. An **open question** is one that calls for the responder to think and then share. Here are two examples: "What more can you tell me about that?" or "What happened in your day?"

A **powerful question** takes that invitation to respond to an even deeper and more thoughtful level of response. Jesus' question to his disciples in Matthew 16:15, "Who do you say that I am?" is a powerful question. It comes in the context of a conversation being held concerning speculation as to his identity. It elicits Peter's famous response: "You are the Christ, the Son of the living God."

Powerful questions in Scripture reflection invite readers to find themselves in the story, and to make personal observations about the story's message for their lives. For example, "Which character do you most identify with in this narrative?" and "What is it about this story's message that speaks to your life?"

One can ask a lot of questions that do little more than rehearse already known information. Or, one can be intentional in asking only a few questions that cause persons to listen, reflect, respond, and grow as disciples and leaders.

Leadership or life coaching is a discipline built around good questions intended to produce forward movement in the lives of those who are being coached. (Additional examples of these different types of questions, including some sample coaching questions, can be found in the appendix of this book.)

Pastors and church leaders engage in leadership activities all of the time, through a wide variety of practices and strategies. While it may transpire through formal or informal coaching, more often leadership happens through the daily and weekly obligations of ministry. Pastors lead through preaching, in pastoral care, by teaching a Bible study or facilitating a small group. Church leaders lead through running team meetings and in working with volunteers to plan church activities and carry out mission projects.

Leadership isn't an activity we engage in separately from our other work. Leadership is part of all of our work. We see this in the life of Jesus. He was always leading people, often through the use of questions, as he encountered and interacted with them.

In the chapters that follow, we will explore eight of the questions Jesus used. This will give us greater insight into how Jesus taught and led others. As you reflect on the questions, and how Jesus posed or responded to them, we hope it will prompt you to consider afresh your own engagement with others in life and ministry. We hope it will cause you to form some questions and use them in your ministry as you lead. We hope you will reexamine your own faith and response to Jesus' questions. We hope you will be encouraged. We hope you will be challenged. We hope you will continue to develop and grow as both a disciple and a leader.

Questions for Group Discussion or Personal Reflection

1. Take a moment to remember some of Jesus' more familiar questions in the Gospels. What question that Jesus asked is most memorable for you? Why?
2. Where in your own personal journey (education, vocation, avocation) have you been exposed to or invited into a growth experience that was centered on questions? What was the outcome of that experience?
3. Consider your current church or ministry context. What one area of ministry would most benefit today

from the use of a few open and powerful questions? What are one or two questions you might pose to others about that ministry?

4. If you were to form an open, powerful question for yourself—given your current chapter or situation of life—what would that question be? How do you respond to it?

Notes

1. This understanding of *midrash* is adapted from Richard Rohr, *Hierarchy of Truths: Jesus' Use of Scripture* (Albuquerque: Center for Action and Contemplation, 2014), CD, MP3 download, http://store.cac.org/Hierarchy-of-Truths-Jesus-Use-of-Scripture-CD_p_334.html.

2. Gary Collins defines coaching as "the art and practice of guiding a person or group from where they are toward the greater competence and fulfillment that they desire" (*Christian Coaching: Helping Others Turn Potential into Reality* [Colorado Springs: NavPress, 2001], 16).

An effective leader will move a person or group forward by asking a powerful question at just the right time.

"Do You Want to Get Well?"

JOHN 5:1-18

SCRIPTURE ENCOUNTER

[1] After this there was a festival of the Jews, and Jesus went up to Jerusalem. [2] Now in Jerusalem by the Sheep Gate there is a pool, called in Hebrew Beth-zatha, which has five porticoes. [3] In these lay many invalids—blind, lame, and paralyzed. [5] One man was there who had been ill for thirty-eight years. [6] When Jesus saw him lying there and knew that he had been there a long time, he said to him, "Do you want to be made well?" [7] The sick man answered him, "Sir, I have no one to put me into the pool when the water is stirred up; and while I am making my way, someone else steps down ahead of me." [8] Jesus said to him, "Stand up, take your mat and walk." [9] At once the man was made well, and he took up his mat and began to walk.

Now that day was a sabbath. [10] So the Jews said to the man who had been cured, "It is the sabbath; it is not lawful for you to carry your mat." [11] But he answered them, "The man who made me well said to me, 'Take up your mat and walk.'" [12] They asked him, "Who is the man who said to you, 'Take it up and walk'?" [13] Now the man who had been healed did not know who it was, for Jesus had disappeared in the crowd that was there. [14] Later Jesus found him in the temple and said to him, "See, you have been made well! Do not sin any more, so that nothing worse happens to you." [15] The man went away and told the Jews that it was Jesus who had made him well. [16] Therefore the Jews started persecuting Jesus, because he was doing such things on the sabbath. [17] But Jesus answered them, "My Father is still working, and I also am working." [18] For this reason the Jews were seeking all the more to kill him, because he was not only breaking the sabbath, but was also calling God his own Father, thereby making himself equal to God.

RELATING TO THE STORY

When did you last feel stuck? Can you recall a time when the circumstances of your life had aligned in such a way that you saw no immediate way forward? A time when in fact you may have felt paralyzed? A time when were you stuck?

This passage from the Gospel of John features a man who was stuck. He was literally unable to move. He was physically disabled and had been in his present physical condition for thirty-eight long years. As we explore his story and the question Jesus asked him, we invite you to think about those times and places in leadership and discipleship when you've felt stuck or when you have been asked to help others move beyond their seemingly limiting circumstances.

In late 2006, as I was approaching a sabbatical study leave, I (Dan) was overwhelmed with feelings of being stuck. I had hit the wall in my professional life and felt it was time to discern a new opportunity in ministry. But the circumstances of my family life did not in any way appear favorable to that, especially if it involved a geographical move. I had three children in school, my oldest in her high school years, and we lived in a community and neighborhood that we truly enjoyed. Furthermore, my wife's widowed mother had recently moved nearby to be close to our family and her younger grandchildren. And my wife had developed a successful small business that was just beginning to come into its own. All of these things appeared to point to our need to remain in the geographical location that we called home. But my vocational opportunities, beyond the current position, were next to nil in that community. I felt stuck.

It was during this time that I benefited from exposure to the concept of leadership coaching. In fact, I was given the opportunity to have my own professional life coach as I learned more about the discipline. The focus of this coaching was mine to determine. What better topic for discussion

> By asking a powerful, open-ended question, you can identify a way forward past obstacles that may have you feeling stuck.

than the predicament at hand? My coach and I talked about my being stuck. Through a series of coaching sessions and open, powerful questions, my coach helped me begin to see the answers that were lying beneath the surface of my thinking and to identify and experience forward movement. Over the next several months, what I had felt was a life stuck in the paralysis of indecision and few options opened up into new opportunities to thrive.

THE QUESTION IN CONTEXT

John 5 tells us that Jesus went to Jerusalem for one of the three Jewish festivals that every Jewish male of the age of twenty or over was required to attend annually. We might note that Jesus appears alone, without his disciples, in this narrative, though we can imagine that they would have been in the city as well. Jesus had come to worship during this festive time, and would likely once again visit the temple in tribute to his faith.

But on this particular occasion, we find him in the city near the Sheep Gate and the nearby pool known as Beth-zatha (NRSV; Bethsaida or Bethesda in other translations). The setting, as described by John, invites our imagination: This pool actually consisted of two large trapezoid-shaped pools with a space between them twenty-one feet in width. The entire structure was enclosed by porches (or covered colonnades), five of them in all.

A large number of persons gathered under these porches at poolside each day. Most of these persons suffered from some form of disability or illness. The text describes the gathering to include those who were blind, lame, and paralyzed (v. 3). This was their daily destination—a gathering place for persons of like situation who found themselves stopped, or paused, by circumstances beyond their control. I'm sure if you were to ask them, many would have said they felt "stuck." So, why were the people there?

Why were the people there?

Legend had it that the water in these pools occasionally was stirred up, perhaps by an underground source such a spring or drainage from another pool. But in the people's minds, this disturbance of the water was connected to a healing power of divine origin, and whoever got into the stirred-up pool first would be cured of whatever infirmity that person suffered. (This legend is recorded in some ancient manuscripts and is included as v. 4 in the footnotes of our Bibles.)

It was their belief in this result that drew people here each day. They came daily—weeks, months, and years at a time—to this location. Fathom that for a moment. What is the mental, the emotional, even the spiritual state of someone who comes for so long? Do they come with hope or with resignation? Is this a daily pilgrimage of faith or an obligatory habit? What kind of community is the group who gathers here? Do they see themselves as outcasts? Desperate? Determined? Has a form of groupthink[1] overtaken them?

It's interesting that Jesus focuses his attention from the many to one man who, we are told, has been an invalid for thirty-eight years (vv. 5-6). Whether the man has come to the pool all of those years, we do not know, but we can speculate that he's a regular. Does he get dropped off there every day? Surely someone, or more than one, must help him arrive. Once present, he appears to be on his own, asserting that he has "no one to put me into the pool when the water is stirred" (v. 7). Clearly, he is stuck, but in what ways?

Given the man's circumstances, Jesus' question "Do you want to get well?" may strike us as a bit direct, if not rude. Who wouldn't want to get well after a lifetime of that kind of suffering? But let's be reminded that paralysis, or at least inertia, comes upon us in many levels and ways. Over those thirty-eight years, this man's physical obstacles may have morphed into an attitude of defeat or a life of resignation. Obstacles have a way of accumulating and multiplying in our thinking. Perhaps all he could see were obstacles, no matter where and how he looked.

Jesus' well-placed, open, and powerful question is not intended to give offense, but rather to awaken the man's self-awareness or redirect his thinking: "*Do* I want to get well? Do I *want* to get well?"

IMPLICATIONS FOR LIFE AND LEADERSHIP

Like a carefully worded coaching question, Jesus' question causes one to see afresh what had not been seen, to dream new dreams that had dried up, to find within self the desire, the hope, the possibility, perhaps even the answer to such a question. Jesus' simple six-word question brought this man to a focal point of decision and self-examination. Did he, or did he not, want to get well?

While I (Bill) was serving on the staff of an inner-city church in 1964, a man came to the door one day at noon and asked me a question: "Mister, would you give me a dime for a cup of coffee?"

I was a little suspicious of what he really wanted to use the dime to purchase, so I said to him, "Since it's lunchtime, how about if I take you to the Good Shepherd Mission and we have lunch together?" The director of the mission was a member of the church and had given me a standing invitation to bring anyone in need of a meal to the mission.

The man replied, "Mister, I only want a dime for a cup of coffee."

I said, "I'm offering to get you as much coffee as you can drink plus a very good warm meal."

He was a bit disappointed and asked, "Mister, are you going to give me a dime for a cup of coffee or not?"

I said, "No, I'm not going to give you a dime, because I'm offering you so much more."

He sadly turned and walked away, and as he walked, he turned and said, "God bless you, mister."

> The opportunity of Jesus' question suggests that there is a way forward to a new or deeper understanding of faith.

This man was stuck by his life circumstances. His refusal of a hot meal and bottomless cup of coffee suggested to me that he was more comfortable with his usual routine—asking for loose change—and remaining in that condition than with accepting an offer that might lead him to consider real change. His answer to my offer to take him to the mission was, in so many words, "No, I don't want to get well."

The opportunities of discipleship, and leadership, often come to us in these poignant moments of decision and determination. In our faith development we may be stuck, at an impasse due to life circumstances. For example, an individual stuck in loss (be it the loss of a job or a relationship) may feel abandoned by God. In this respect, that person's faith development is at something of an impasse. However, the opportunity of Jesus' question suggests that there is a way forward to a new or deeper understanding of faith. By answering, "Yes, I want to get well (move forward)," a person becomes open to discerning how faith may guide life beyond the present.

In this respect, such places become crossroads from which we will either move forward or regress. Given the challenges, we might be asking ourselves, "Do I want to move forward?" "Do I wish to grow deeper?" "Do I want to trust Christ's leadership and guidance?" When we affirm, like this man at the pool, that yes, we do want to become more than stuck, it's surprising how often things begin to loosen up in our thinking, and how new depth of faith can take root.

As leaders, we will arrive at this crossroads of decision, both within our roles as leaders and with those whom we lead. Do we, will we, press on and do the hard work of leading, or will we retreat or, worse yet, settle for whatever may amount to collecting dimes?

In such times, Jesus' question comes to us with a simple and direct jolt intended to promote self-examination of conscience. To answer yes is to invite the next question, which is also to invite forward movement and thus refuse to yield to being stuck.

A FINAL WORD

Notice that the actions Jesus takes on this day, as leader, healer, and prophet, subsequently cause him difficulty with others (vv. 16-18). He is criticized for healing on the Sabbath and for directing this man to carry his bed on the Sabbath day. This was an offense under the law, punishable by stoning (Numbers 15:32-36). "Will you challenge the status quo?"

Like the persons gathered poolside, many might respond with honesty: "To change is too hard, too frightening, too painful. I'll stick with what I know." But others will take up the challenge to lead, to answer the question in the affirmative, which then will bring the next question and release imagination and hope, in the community.

Congregations today are facing issues that are potentially disturbing to those members who are content with the status quo. Worship styles have taken on labels of being "traditional or contemporary." We challenge the status quo of church membership requiring baptism by immersion, when it is suggested that one's faith commitment is not about the amount of water used. The status quo contentment with women having a lesser role of importance in church leadership is challenged by ordaining women and by changing church by-laws to permit women to serve in any elected church position, as well as being considered to fill a pastoral vacancy.

Numerous cultural issues have caused individuals, churches, and denominations to examine their long-held beliefs. Issues related to lesbian, gay, bisexual, transgender, and gender-queer (LGBTQ) individuals are not only battles being waged in state legislatures and in the courts; they also are of concern to individuals and congregations. Local congregations are also addressing issues of immigration, gun control, and mass incarceration that have taken center stage in politics. These social issues, among others, provide individual leaders and disciples the opportunity to examine how the issues may affect their personal faith commitment.

In addition to the religious and social issues that each of us must process, there are the personal issues that only the individual knows about that may be a challenge to the status quo. Addictions that are difficult to admit, broken relationships that are difficult to repair, and grief experiences that are slow to heal may keep us stuck in ways such that we conclude that we "don't want to get well."

Where does this question that Jesus asked find you today? What might be your response to the question "Do you want to get well?"

Questions for Group Discussion or Personal Reflection

Please read John 5:1-18.

1. With whom do you identify in this story? Why?
2. When have you been "stuck" or paralyzed in a situation and someone's question challenged your thinking or helped you to reexamine your circumstances?
3. How might you attempt to avoid being responsible for being stuck?
4. How might this man's encounter with Jesus have caused him to question other things in his life? What does one question unleash?
5. How would you respond to Jesus' question "Do you want to get well?" Why?

Notes

1. "*Groupthink* is a term first used in 1972 by social psychologist Irving L. Janis that refers to a psychological phenomenon in which people strive for consensus within a group. In many cases, people will set aside their own personal beliefs or adopt the opinion of the rest of the group" (Kendra Cherry, "What Is Groupthink?" June 14, 2016, http://psychology.about.com/od/gindex/g/groupthink.htm).

A few years ago I met an old professor at the University of Notre Dame. Looking back on his long life of teaching, he said with a funny twinkle in his eyes, "I have always been complaining that my work was constantly interrupted, until I slowly discovered that my interruptions were my work."[1]

2

"Who Touched My Clothes?"

MARK 5:21-43

SCRIPTURE ENCOUNTER

[21] When Jesus had crossed again in the boat to the other side, a great crowd gathered around him; and he was by the sea. [22] Then one of the leaders of the synagogue named Jairus came and, when he saw him, fell at his feet [23] and begged him repeatedly, "My little daughter is at the point of death. Come and lay your hands on her, so that she may be made well, and live." [24] So he went with him.

And a large crowd followed him and pressed in on him. [25] Now there was a woman who had been suffering from hemorrhages for twelve years. [26] She had endured much under many physicians, and had spent all that she had; and she was no better, but rather grew worse. [27] She had heard about Jesus, and came up behind him in the crowd and touched his cloak, [28] for she said, "If I but touch his clothes, I will be made well." [29] Immediately her hemorrhage stopped; and she felt in her body that she was healed of her disease. [30] Immediately aware that power had gone forth from him, Jesus turned about in the crowd and said, "Who touched my clothes?" [31] And his disciples said to him, "You see the crowd pressing in on you; how can you say, 'Who touched me?'" [32] He looked all around to see who had done it. [33] But the woman, knowing what had happened to her, came in fear and trembling, fell down before him, and told him the whole truth. [34] He said to her, "Daughter, your faith has made you well; go in peace, and be healed of your disease."

[35] While he was still speaking, some people came from the leader's house to say, "Your daughter is dead. Why trouble the teacher any further?" [36] But overhearing what they said, Jesus said to the leader of the synagogue, "Do not fear, only believe." [37] He allowed no one to follow him except Peter, James, and John, the brother of James. [38] When they came to the house of the leader of the synagogue, he saw a commotion, people weeping and wailing loudly. [39] When he had entered, he said to them, "Why do you make a commotion and weep? The child is not dead but sleeping." [40] And they laughed at him. Then he put them all outside, and took the child's father and mother and those who were with him, and went in where the child was. [41] He took her by the hand and said to her, "Talitha cum," which means, "Little girl, get up!" [42] And immediately the girl got up and began to walk about (she was twelve years of age). At this they were overcome with amazement. [43] He strictly ordered them that no one should know this, and told them to give her something to eat.

RELATING TO THE STORY

We all have had days when what we had planned to do is continuously interrupted by what demands our attention. I (Dan) remember a day not long ago when I fielded multiple requests for my time and attention. A respected lay leader in the church was going to be honored at a community reception, which I planned to attend. At the very last minute, I was asked to share some remarks of recognition and appreciation at the event. There was an urgency to this request compounded by that leader's failing health and his peers' sense of grief and desire to honor him.

Meanwhile my afternoon plans already included a pastoral care visit to a couple who were adjusting to news of a health crisis, and my need to run a personal errand that was time-sensitive. While in the midst of those planned endeavors I received two phone calls, each of which went to voicemail. One was from a person I had been counseling who was in the midst of a crisis and wanted to see me that day. The second call was notifying me of a death and asking that I return the call.

As these requests (planned and unplanned) piled up, I began to feel the stress of that busy day and took note of how my emotions were triggering both physical and mental responses. I also noted that the requests coming my way were not neutral but carried the emotions of those who made them. My awareness of these factors, and the ability to name them, helped me form a triage plan for response in both my thinking and actions. The day was truly an example of the interruptions becoming my work.

> Leaders know the reality of interruption.

Leaders know the reality of interruption. We can start a day with our very best and most organized plan of action only to see that plan go out the window because of the interruptions caused by working with and leading others. We may have the creative ability and flexibility to reorganize our plan, but we must also factor in how the physical and emotional responses involved will impact our decisions and actions. We see all of this at play in Jesus as he interacts with multiple persons and their requests in Mark 4–5, and as he pauses along the way to ask, "Who touched my clothes?"

THE QUESTION IN CONTEXT

It is helpful to look back through Mark 4–5 in order to understand and appreciate the significance of Jesus' words and actions in 5:21-43. As we do so, we see that Jesus has already spent an entire day teaching a very large crowd from a boat that was anchored seaside (Mark 4:1). When evening came, he and the disciples took leave of that crowd, sailing for the other side of the Sea of Galilee (Mark 4:35). Once they were on board, Jesus' physical fatigue overtook him, and he went to the back of the boat to sleep. But his sleep was interrupted by frantic disciples certain that a fast-arising storm was about to swamp their boat and endanger their lives.

Once they arrived safely on the other side, any hope Jesus had of a respite from the demands of crowds was crushed by an encounter with a demon-possessed man. One can only imagine the toll an exorcism took on Jesus as he confronted this man and released him from the torment of his demonic possession. Added to this was the paranoia of a crowd, uncertain as to what to do with someone as powerful as Jesus; the respite he hoped for in the region of the Gerasenes was nixed for a return across the lake.

It is here we pick up the story in Mark 5:21, as Jesus lands to the welcome of another great crowd and the immediate need of Jairus, one of the leaders of the synagogue. Imagine yourself in his situation. You've had very little sleep in a twenty-four-hour period. You've been teaching and speaking at length publicly, and then engaged in some very intense interpersonal and spiritual work (exorcism), and you've had a large crowd of people watching your every move. Are you ready at this moment to receive yet another request for assistance? Do you welcome Jairus and his personal family crisis? How do you manage all that is going on around you and within you and the ever-present crowd that now accompanies you wherever you go? How do you get anything done with all of these interruptions?

IMPLICATIONS FOR LIFE AND LEADERSHIP

Before we follow the story further, this is a good place to pause and acknowledge the necessity for leaders to cultivate their awareness and management of emotional responses to the demands of leading. The capacity for such awareness and management is better known as emotional intelligence quotient, or

EQ. Emotional intelligence is the ability to recognize and understand emotions, and an EQ test measures an individual's skill at using this awareness to manage emotions in oneself and in one's relationships with others.[2]

> Just as we all have an IQ, so we each have an EQ.

Just as we all have an IQ (intelligence quotient), so we each have an EQ. But whereas one's IQ is static and doesn't change over time, your EQ is much less static and something you can work on and improve. EQ is a topic within leadership that recognizes the importance of a leader being self-aware as well as other-aware in order to manage his or her response to situations and groups. The following table illustrates the four quadrants of EQ:

Emotional Intelligence Quotient Quadrants

Self-Awareness	Self-Management
Watch and observe what you are feeling.	Note your first reaction (E), and don't let E hijack you.
Social Awareness	**Social Management**
Watch and recognize moods of others as they react.	Use self-awareness, self-management, and social awareness as you respond to others.

As we consider the physical and emotional demands upon Jesus during the period described in Mark 4–5, we are focusing our attention on his first quadrant: self-awareness. In this quadrant we learn to watch and observe ourselves—what we are feeling, how we are reacting. After a long boat ride, continuous days of being in the midst of crowds, and the emotionally draining work of exorcism of the demons who tortured the man who lived in the Gerasene tombs, Jesus' awareness of his emotions would become key to his ability to manage those feelings.

Self-management is the second quadrant of EQ. It builds on the work of awareness by refusing to allow emotions to hijack one's reaction, but rather choosing a more appropriate and helpful response. For example, if a leader's initial response to an interruption is annoyance and he or she allows that to be seen and known, the person interrupting will have received a dominant message that is difficult to overlook. However, if a leader is aware of the tendency to be annoyed when interrupted, but manages that reaction by substituting a response of curiosity, the outcome of the encounter may be much different.

The example of Jesus throughout this story is of a leader who functions at the highest level of EQ, illustrating for us what may be possible if we will practice our own self-awareness and self-management. We notice in Mark 5:24 that Jesus doesn't rebuff Jairus with any words, a yawn, sigh, or roll of the eyes, but "he went with him." How was that possible? Well, we might say it was possible because we are talking about Jesus, after all. But Jesus was human and subject to fatigue. It's more likely he was also a leader who was self-aware and so able to manage his response to others in such a way as to overcome the initial emotional or physical response that may have proven harmful or disingenuous.

The encounter that Jesus has with Jairus, and the subsequent interruption of his mission to go home with him and heal his daughter, will illustrate the final two quadrants of EQ.

BACK TO THE QUESTION IN CONTEXT

Imagine the emotions of a father who is desperate to help and find relief for his seriously ill twelve-year-old girl. The illness of a child gets the attention of any parent and the extended family. Does Mark include the status of Jairus, as a leader of the synagogue, to further demonstrate his willingness that day to humiliate himself as he begs Jesus for intervention? We can almost feel the raw emotion of this desperate man as he falls at Jesus' feet and repeatedly begs him to come and lay hands on his daughter. How could Jesus, a man who repeatedly takes compassion on those in need, refuse such a request? He puts aside his weariness and accompanies Jairus on the road toward home.

But the situation grows more complex by the moment. Here comes another interruption! This time Jesus becomes aware of the significant touch of one in the surrounding crowd who seeks healing. Mark's narration gives us the understory. A woman who has suffered from hemorrhages for twelve years, who has spent her life savings seeking answers and cures from doctors, and who is desperate to be made well reaches out to touch Jesus' cloak. In that simple act of faith, healing is released from Jesus to the woman. But why the need to draw attention to it? Why does Jesus stop? Why does he ask his question: "Who touched my clothes?"

Certainly we could argue that the woman is the cause of this latest interruption, but doesn't some of the credit go to Jesus? He's the one who feels compelled to stop and address the situation. Jesus is the one who stalls the procession to Jairus's home, choosing instead to be in the moment with the woman. Why?

> Jesus is not just bringing attention to this woman and her faith; he is also announcing her value.

We both have had admiration for leaders who know how important it is to be present with those who need personal attention. Such priority, often at the expense of a next appointment, conveys value to the one being listened to and addressed. Think how different such undivided attention feels as opposed to an encounter with a leader who is always looking ahead to who may be next.

By stopping the procession and asking his question, Jesus is not just bringing attention to this woman and her faith; he is also announcing her value. One who, by virtue of the law, has been unclean for twelve years is now proclaimed clean. One who, by virtue of her gender, has often gone unnoticed—and even here is unnamed—is noticed and affirmed. As she meekly comes before Jesus in response to his query, "Who touched my clothes?" the woman is acknowledged by him with the affectionate address "daughter." A story that is all about a desperate intervention for Jairus's daughter includes the healing of this adult daughter of God. Her faith has made her well, and she is told to go in peace. It may be the first peace she has known in twelve years.

But there's not much peace among the crowd, the disciples, or with Jairus and his household. This delay, and Jesus' question, has become the cause of great consternation. "What do you mean, 'Who touched me?'" the disciples ask. "You can see this crowd pressing in on you!"

Emotion is ruling the day. Emotion is wrung from an ever-growing and uneasy crowd, from a father (and synagogue leader) desperate for action and frustrated with Jesus' delay while he addresses such a marginal person, and then from news that it's too late—Jairus's daughter is now dead (v. 35). The delay of a question appears to have been enough to thwart the hoped-for outcome of a desperate father and his friends.

MORE IMPLICATIONS FOR LIFE AND LEADERSHIP

In this portion of the story we watch Jesus engage in the final two quadrants of EQ: social awareness and social management. In quadrant three, social awareness, a leader observes and recognizes the emotional response of others. Jesus' disciples' response to the interruption is filled with emotion. They are incredulous at such a seemingly foolish question, given the pressing crowd. They are also aware that time spent chasing after such questions is inhibiting the prior mission of response to a synagogue leader's need.

When the woman finally emerges from the crowd, Jesus assesses her mood and needs. One could argue that he's forced into a situation of leader triage. Which need takes priority, the prior urgent need of the synagogue ruler and his daughter, or the emergent need he's now facing in the person of this woman?

A leader who has not engaged in the EQ work of self-awareness, self-management, and social awareness is not prepared to enter the final quadrant of social management and to make such a triage decision. It's in this fourth quadrant of EQ that all of the information garnered from the other three quadrants comes into play as an informed and balanced response is made.

Note that as this story evolves, Jesus continues in the leadership work of EQ. He has to be aware of the emotions at play in his own person, and those surfacing in the group. And he then has to manage all of the above. He does this as he redirects Jairus to his home and daughter, clears the room of mourners, and takes the child by the hand and calls her to "get up" (v. 41).

Jesus' calm and measured approach to each party in this elongated story made it possible for him to continue engagement with each one. He did not allow their emotions to hijack his decisions or actions. He managed both his internal (personal) and external (social) response and thereby continued to be effective in his interactions with all. This allowed him to give priority to what he judged to be an immediate need (the woman with the hemorrhage), while staying engaged with what was equally significant (the situation with Jairus's daughter).

When leaders practice such obvious discipline and thoughtfully managed responses to the multiple demands and interruptions on their time, those whom they lead will be more generally able to understand and accept their actions.

However, staying in good communication with all those in the process is essential if it is to be understood.

Two women were healed that day—a twelve-year-old girl and a woman who had been ill for twelve years. Two women were healed—two who experienced the touch of Jesus, who allowed himself to be interrupted. Two women were healed, but many others had their lives changed by the work of one who came among them as a leader, a teacher, and Savior.

When have you faced similar interruptions in your life and leadership? When have you been torn between two or more choices (requests or expectations), each of which was important? How did you respond?

> **When have you been torn between two or more choices?**

I (Bill) remember such an occasion that surfaced one Christmas season. It was the Sunday before Christmas, with Christmas being on Wednesday that year. I had already preached at the 9:30 a.m. service at First Baptist Church Columbus, and then at the 11:00 a.m. chapel service at the Baptist retirement home, as well as the 1:00 p.m. Health Center chapel service. This was my weekly schedule, and on Sunday afternoons I was very tired and would normally fall asleep watching a football game.

When I woke from my nap on that December Sunday, my wife reminded me that we needed to get ready to go Christmas caroling with the church group at 6:00 p.m. It wasn't what I wanted to do that evening, but I really had no choice but to support the effort. So we went.

We got home about 8:00 p.m., and I put on my pajamas and fell asleep in front of the television. Waking up about 9:30 p.m., I went to bed. At 11:00 p.m. the telephone rang. When I answered it, a man's voice asked me if I was the pastor, and I said yes. He proceeded to tell me that he and his wife were traveling to northern Indiana for Christmas and had car trouble on Interstate 65 and needed help. He needed a place to stay and a place to get his car repaired.

I knew that our local Salvation Army or Love Chapel agencies were not available at that hour of the night. He told me he was at the Waffle House just off of I-65. I knew the place, and I told him that I'd be there as soon as possible.

The temperature was below freezing and the ground was snow-covered. I got dressed and went to the Waffle House. My attitude was one of "Why me? How did he get my phone number?" On the way I began to wonder how I was going to help them. I did have an agreement with a local motel that would provide rooms for such persons and bill the church, so I thought that this would solve the overnight need. I also knew that there was a gas station near my home that did good repair work on automobiles.

When I arrived at the Waffle House, I could see through the fogged-up windows two persons sitting at the counter. I went in and identified myself, and they introduced themselves and told me their story. The couple was in their late teen-age years and she was six months pregnant. I asked them if they had eaten lately, and they said they had not, so I bought them each a meal. I had coffee, and we talked about their problem. I offered them overnight lodging and suggested that we would deal with the car in the morning. They were very thankful for the offer.

The next morning, I picked them up at 8:00 a.m. and took them to the gas station. We talked with the owner, explaining the problem, and he said he would send a tow truck to pick up the car. The man identified the car and where it was parked at the Waffle House and gave the car keys to the driver. I took the couple to a local restaurant and we ate breakfast together. All this time, I knew I needed to be back in my office making preparations for our Christmas Eve service and was frustrated by having my schedule interrupted. The motel agreed that the couple could stay in the room until the car was repaired, so I dropped them off and told them I would get a call when the car was ready and pick them up.

About 11:30 a.m. I got a call saying that the car was repaired, so I went and picked them up and took them to get the car. The station owner said he would bill the church for the repair, but he was not charging them the full price. We thanked him for his speedy service, filled up the tank with gasoline, and I gave the couple thirty dollars.

The couple left, and I went back to my office to prepare a Christmas Eve message. I didn't like being so far behind because of the interruption over the past twelve hours. As I sat at my desk and began to think about the text I had chosen for the sermon, I couldn't get this couple off my mind. Then it suddenly dawned upon me that they were the Christmas message: a young pregnant couple looking for lodging.

A Consistent Pattern

The stories of Jesus' ministry to and with Jairus and of the woman healed of her hemorrhage may most clearly identify his ability to see the value in the interruptions of life. But it is not the only time we find Jesus advocating such thoughts. One could argue that the parable of the good Samaritan makes the same point, and one could point to multiple other occasions in Jesus' ministry when he stopped and allowed himself to be in the moment with someone, even though other matters called for his attention.

One way to grapple with this story and the challenge of seeing interruptions as opportunity is by asking yourself which of the persons in the story you identify with most. If you are a project- or task-driven person, you may identify with the disciples, who are a bit put out with Jesus for allowing himself to be delayed. If you are not one to draw attention to yourself, you may understand the woman's behavior. If you know what it is to be responsible for the welfare of a child, it may be Jairus who catches your attention most.

Regardless, it's likely that each of us can find ourself in the story. Just as it is also likely we each know the reality of being interrupted.

Practical Matters

Personality types seldom change, and some are more readily open to interruptions (some even hope for them). Knowing your own type therefore is a key to understanding how you can accommodate the good in interruptions while also staying true to how you work and lead best.

If, for example, you are a focused and task-oriented person who also values being open to your team and those you lead, you may wish to keep an open-door policy during office hours, but arrive early to focus on those key tasks before others arrive at the office. The point is that one can grow to appreciate and embrace the best of being interrupted without completely sacrificing work or leadership habits that have served you well.

One of the most difficult areas to manage when it comes to interruptions and leadership (especially in ministry contexts) is when the interruption makes demands on personal or family plans. How many times has a pastor had a death or other congregational emergency come up just as a planned vacation rolled around on the calendar? Or, how often does a meeting conflict with a leader's need to attend his or her own child's or grandchild's event?

Learning to circumnavigate these kinds of leadership challenges is an ongoing task worth consideration. Boundaries for the benefit of family and personal life are important. But there are times when the emergent need will trump even those boundaries. Having a backup plan in place, knowing whom to point persons to when you are not available, and making every effort to recover lost time with family after the fact form a good preventative practice when this occurs.

Jesus' question, "Who touched my clothes?" was not born from his reluctance to be touched. On the contrary Jesus wanted to know who touched him so that he could respond to that person's need. Compassionate leaders are always touching the lives of others, which is why interruptions are seen as an opportunity to further engage in that work. In fact, we might say, interruptions are the work.

Questions for Group Discussion or Personal Reflection

Please read Mark 5:21-43.

1. Which of the persons in the Scripture passage do you identify with the most? Why?
2. How do you generally respond to interruptions that disrupt your plans?
3. Refer to the table on page 25, "Emotional Intelligence Quotient Quadrants." Which of the emotional intelligence quotient quadrants do you find it easiest to engage? Share an example of a time you consciously practiced working on your EQ.
4. Consider all of the interruptions found in Mark 4–5. What physical and/or emotional toll might each one have on a leader? Which one(s) might be most taxing on you?
5. When have you faced interruptions in your life or leadership where you were torn between two or more choices, each of which was important? How did you respond?
6. What other stories in the Gospels illustrate Jesus responding to interruptions with grace, calm, compassion, and an opportunity for ministry?

Notes

1. Henri J. M. Nouwen, *Out of Solitude: Three Meditations on the Christian Life* (Notre Dame, IN: Ave Maria Press, 2004), 56.

2. The concept of emotional intelligence quotient presented in this chapter has been shared by various authors, including Travis Bradberry and Jean Greaves, *The Emotional Intelligence Quick Book: Everything You Need to Know to Put Your EQ to Work* (New York: Simon & Schuster, 2005).

Authority is a lot like a bar of soap: the more you use it, the less you have.

3

"What Do You Want Me to Do for You?"

MARK 10:32-52

SCRIPTURE ENCOUNTER

[32] They were on the road, going up to Jerusalem, and Jesus was walking ahead of them; they were amazed, and those who followed were afraid. He took the twelve aside again and began to tell them what was to happen to him, [33] saying, "See, we are going up to Jerusalem, and the Son of Man will be handed over to the chief priests and the scribes, and they will condemn him to death; then they will hand him over to the Gentiles; [34] they will mock him, and spit upon him, and flog him, and kill him; and after three days he will rise again."

[35] James and John, the sons of Zebedee, came forward to him and said to him, "Teacher, we want you to do for us whatever we ask of you." [36] And he said to them, "What is it you want me to do for you?" [37] And they said to him, "Grant us to sit, one at your right hand and one at your left, in your glory." [38] But Jesus said to them, "You do not know what you are asking. Are you able to drink the cup that I drink, or be baptized with the baptism that I am baptized with?" [39] They replied, "We are able." Then Jesus said to them, "The cup that I drink you will drink; and with the baptism with which I am baptized, you will be baptized; [40] but to

sit at my right hand or at my left is not mine to grant, but it is for those for whom it has been prepared."

[41] When the ten heard this, they began to be angry with James and John. [42] So Jesus called them and said to them, "You know that among the Gentiles those whom they recognize as their rulers lord it over them, and their great ones are tyrants over them. [43] But it is not so among you; but whoever wishes to become great among you must be your servant, [44] and whoever wishes to be first among you must be slave of all. [45] For the Son of Man came not to be served but to serve, and to give his life a ransom for many."

[46] They came to Jericho. As he and his disciples and a large crowd were leaving Jericho, Bartimaeus son of Timaeus, a blind beggar, was sitting by the roadside. [47] When he heard that it was Jesus of Nazareth, he began to shout out and say, "Jesus, Son of David, have mercy on me!" [48] Many sternly ordered him to be quiet, but he cried out even more loudly, "Son of David, have mercy on me!" [49] Jesus stood still and said, "Call him here." And they called the blind man, saying to him, "Take heart; get up, he is calling you." [50] So throwing off his cloak, he sprang up and came to Jesus. [51] Then Jesus said to him, "What do you want me to do for you?" The blind man said to him, "My teacher, let me see again." [52] Jesus said to him, "Go; your faith has made you well." Immediately he regained his sight and followed him on the way.

THE QUESTION IN CONTEXT

Beware of those who come to faith and leadership for all the wrong reasons. That might be the annotated summary offered for the first part of this passage from Mark 10. In the text (vv. 32-52), Jesus' question, "What do you want me to do for you?" is asked twice in different, yet related, contexts—first to two disciples who have been in leadership training with Jesus for the past three years, and later to a blind man who asks for physical sight and gains much more.

James and John

In the first story, James and John, the sons of Zebedee, appear to be leaders overcome with their own agenda. They have a very clear picture in mind of what Jesus can do for them, and it begins with reserved seating in the kingdom.

It's tempting to demonize the brothers' grasp for power. However, few of us are pure when it comes to our own reasoning in the pursuit of authority and the practice of discipleship. There is an allure and flattery that sometimes accompanies positions of leadership. We see it when a lay leader likes the microphone a little too much, or when a person new to preaching measures success solely on the number of "good sermon" comments made at the door. It is a temptation as old as organization: to wield authority based on position, to mistake opportunity as permission for ambition, or to join a church for the business contacts.

> Could it really be that they weren't listening?

By the time James and John boldly respond to Jesus' question, stating what he can do for them (v. 37), they seem to have missed hearing him teach them three times about his coming passion. Mark 10 tells us that the disciples and Jesus were on their way up to Jerusalem. It's a journey that will take them through Jericho and past a blind man named Bartimaeus, culminating in the final Passover that Jesus will celebrate with his disciples. The roads must be crowded with travelers, and there are plenty of distractions. At least, the two Sons of Thunder (see Mark 3:17) appear to be distracted.

Could it really be that they weren't listening? Didn't they hear Jesus say, not once or twice, but three times (Mark 8:31-33; 9:30-32; 10:33-34) that he was soon to be betrayed, be handed over to suffer, and be killed? It's amazing what you can tune out when you are solely focused on your own personal ambition.

It may be that they, along with Peter, as part of the inner circle of disciples, felt some entitlement to privilege and position. What seems certain is that they were operating with a different understanding of authority than Jesus had. For them, authority was related to position. To sit at Jesus' left and right, the power seats, would solidify both their authority and their position. For Jesus, however, leadership and authority were based on service and trust.

In his patient response to the two brothers, Jesus continues to teach them. He uses two common Jewish metaphors: the cup and baptism. According to William Barclay in his Bible study commentary on Mark's Gospel, the cup is a metaphor for "the life and experience that God handed out."[1] "Baptism," here in its verbal form, "to baptize," means "to submerge," and it is a metaphor for the experience of being immersed in the coming hatred, pain, and death that await Jesus. "Can you drink this cup (life experience) and be baptized with this baptism (death)?" Jesus asks. "We can," comes the response. Really? No lack of confidence, these two! Rather than give them pause, Jesus' words seem to be taken as challenge, and they pronounce themselves ready.

It's interesting that their fellow disciples are less enthusiastic when it comes to the self-claimed coronation of James and John. In fact, they are disgusted. Indignant! We are reminded of this old adage: "Authority is a lot like a bar of soap: the more you use it, the less you have." Perhaps the other ten were tired of these two colleagues jockeying for position and authority—or perhaps they were just disappointed that they had not thought to ask for the power seats first.

Jesus' teaching (vv. 42-45) turns their understanding of authority and leadership on its head. He says nothing of position or the pursuit of accolades. He lifts up the servant leader, the one who would become the least, the slave of all.

IMPLICATIONS FOR LIFE AND LEADERSHIP

Young and inexperienced leaders benefit from strong mentors and models when it comes to learning about authority and leadership. Dan would have that experience in learning from the man who would become his father-in-law. Charles Kline, known as "Sonny" to his friends and "Mr. K" to the young men and women who served on his summer camp staff, was a quiet and unassuming man. He led and worked with a servant's heart, often doing the behind-the-scenes jobs at a camp that no one else wanted to do. This included unplugging the toilets, digging out the septic systems, and responding to late night and early morning calls for assistance and support from camp directors and cabin leaders.

Mr. K's generally stoic personality and ability to navigate life, while using few words, led some to misread him as gruff or harsh. In truth, he was a tenderhearted servant. Though he could don a suit and tie and give a presentation on camp to any supporting church, he was most comfortable in his work boots, faded t-shirt, and jeans, doing the necessary and needed support work to keep ministry flowing and the camp functioning smoothly. He modeled a strong work ethic and servant style to the many young people who worked on his staff over several summers. How did he manage that? Those who sought the limelight were often given equal opportunity to share in the grunt work of the next day. Message sent. Message received.

> Young and inexperienced leaders benefit from strong mentors and models.

At the end of a long work day, which began well before the sun rose, you would often find Mr. K seated in the back row of the camp chapel, listening, watching, and worshiping right along with the young people and their program leaders. Tears would sometimes stream down his face as he found reward in the labor and watched young people come to a deeper Christian faith.

Perhaps you have a mentor or model in your own life's journey who helped you see leadership and authority from a behind-the-scenes viewpoint. Maybe this person even tempered your grasp for the power seats. For James and John, that model was Jesus.

BACK TO THE QUESTION IN CONTEXT

Bartimaeus—A Man Born Blind

As Mark continues the narrative (vv. 46-52), we continue on the road to Jerusalem, a road traveled by pilgrims over the generations, a road known for its less-than-hospitable terrain and risks to travelers. It is along this road that we hear the second occurrence of Jesus' question: "What do you want me to do for you?"

Sitting by the roadside, begging, a blind man named Bartimaeus responds to the sounds of the crowd and news of Jesus being present. He begins to call out, "Son of David, have mercy on me!"

Jesus stops!

His plea in itself might surprise us. Passover travel season would have been one of the more lucrative times of the year for someone such as Bartimaeus, whose only source of income was begging. The increased traffic and sacred purpose for which persons went to Jerusalem would have meant an increase in his income. To set the begging aside and call out to a distant Jesus indicates a true desire for an encounter.

The crowd does its best to shush the beggar. They rebuke him and tell him to be quiet, but he will not. He knows what he needs. He understands who is present. He is desperate to be heard. And Jesus stops.

Jesus stops! Imagine this. Jesus stops. Given what he has been doing, where he is going, what may be on his mind, Jesus, the servant leader, stops. He was willing to be interrupted. He found ministry in the interruptions. So he stops and asks Bartimaeus, "What do you want me to do for you?"

I (Bill) remember in my early years as a youth minister in Paterson, New Jersey, a particular day when I was in a hurry to get back to the church office. I had taken the church van to be serviced, and it took longer than I had planned. I had a list of things I had to get done for the coming youth retreat so that the secretary could make copies before she left for the day. It was around 2:00 p.m. when I parked the van and walked toward the back door of the church. As I approached the door, I noticed a small African American boy, about six years old, sitting on the steps at the back door. He was alone and should have been in school, so I wondered why he was sitting there. My first thought was that I didn't have time to stop and have any conversation with him, but the closer I got, the more he stared at me. I thought I'd better stop and be friendly.

As I got near the door, he moved away from the center of the steps to the side so I could enter. Instead, I decided to sit down next to him. We sat in silence for a moment or two, a young black child and a white young adult, and then I said, "My name is Bill."

He looked up at me and said, "Hi."

A few more moments of silence passed, and he continued to look up at me, so I asked him, "What's your name?"

He said, "Freddie."

He continued to look up at me, not making eye contact, but looking above my eyes at the top of my head. I finally asked, "What are you looking at?"

He said, "Mister, you sure have funny hair."

I smiled and thought how often I had thought that those of his race also had funny hair, but I never had the courage to express it. Since he was being so honest, I said, "Freddie, I think you're the one with the funny hair."

He laughed and said, "My hair's not funny. Yours is funny."

In those fleeting moments, I realized that this was a moment for both of us to have a new experience, so I risked asking him, "Would you like to touch my hair?"

His eyes got big and he smiled, and after thinking about it he said, "Yeah."

I said, "I'll let you touch my hair if you let me touch yours."

He said, "OK."

There we sat on the back step of the church with my head bent low so he could reach my hair with his hands. I put my hands on his head as his fingers moved slowly and gently through my hair. We smiled at each other and after a minute or two we stopped.

I asked, "Do you still think my hair is funny?"

He said, "No, mister, it's soft."

"I don't think your hair is funny either," I said.

He suddenly stood up and said, "Gotta go, mister. Bye."

"Nice meeting you, Freddie."

I've often thought of how much I would have missed if I had not stopped. This was back in the 1960s, when racial differences were in all the newspaper headlines; but for one young boy and me, it was a moment of sharing, and our eyes were opened to see the other in a new light. I never spoke with the boy again, although he waved to me when he rode his bike through the church parking lot. I can't help but wonder if I made as much a difference in his life as he has in mine.

MORE IMPLICATIONS FOR
LIFE AND LEADERSHIP

How many times have you, as a leader—as a disciple—been too busy to stop? When have you stopped, even though you were busy, but not regretted it? Some of the most meaningful ministry moments can occur when and because we stop.

Jesus stopped. The blind man was brought to him and Jesus asked him the same question that he had asked James and John: "What do you want me to do for you?"

"Teacher, I want to see." This request, so different from the response of James and John, doesn't come from a place of power seeking. This is a direct prayer for a particular need. It is presented in faith. If only he could be in the presence of Jesus. If only he could speak with this teacher and healer, the opportunity for sight would be granted.

Jesus used the same question in both encounters, yet it was received so very differently. What a contrast between the response of Bartimaeus and the request made by James and John. James and John were interested in selfish ambition and were therefore "blind" to Jesus' purpose, yet the blind man could "see" in Jesus one who was like David of old, and he believed that Jesus' words could make a difference in his life.

We continue to see how the same question can elicit different responses today. During my tenure as a regional judicatory minister (the job title was Area Resource Minister), I (Dan) often fielded what I came to designate "Monday calls" from pastors and church leaders. The content of these calls often concerned something that happened in a congregation on Sunday that left someone upset. (The vote at the congregational meeting did not go their way. The sermon was too critical or too personally criticized. Conflict erupted between leaders in some fashion.) My stock question during those phone conversations often came back to "How can I best help you in this situation?"—a version of "What do you want me to do for you?"

Responses, of course, varied. Some, like James and John, wanted me to come in and fix it—"it" being their predetermined outcome. Others didn't want me to do anything but listen and allow them to vent. Still others just needed the perspective of someone not so personally engaged in the situation, and they appreciated my coaching questions guiding them toward their own next step. A few, like Bartimaeus, were more than ready to answer my question with their own hope for sight—a brighter future filled with the hope of Christ. They wanted to know and experience the mercy and grace of Jesus in their life and faith community.

When we absorb it fully, the question "What do you want me to do for you?" causes us to stop and consider the future and our role in it, whether as a leader or disciple, in relationship to Christ.

As a leader, you will be faced with those who make requests, wanting you to do something for them. Some of these requests attempt to barter favors for decisions. In the political arena, this is called lobbying, and it is accepted as an appropriate use of power or leverage. It is often exercised in church life as well when a person attempts to use influence, whether personal or financial, to ensure that a leader will make the "right" decision, which favors that individual's own wishes.

Preachers tell an old story about the two brothers who were church members. One brother, who was known around town as the brother who loved his booze and his women, died. His surviving brother went to the pastor and said, "Regarding Bob's funeral, there is something I want you to do for me. At the funeral I want you to say, 'Bob was a saint.'" The pastor said that would be very difficult to do. The brother said, "If you will do it, I'll donate $50,000 to the new church building fund." The pastor said, "Let me think about that." The next day at the funeral the pastor came to the eulogy for Bob and made this opening statement: "We're here to celebrate Bob's life. Compared to his brother, Bob was a saint!"

It's only a story, but the nugget of truth is that persons do approach leaders with requests that will show favoritism for some form of trade-off.

I (Bill) remember several times in my years of ministry that I was informed through "back-channels" that I should promote a certain decision before the church, or else a certain member was either going to leave the church or cut his or her financial giving. On one occasion, the week after I became pastor of the church, I was invited out to be a guest for lunch by a corporation executive. I was suspicious of his intent, and during the luncheon he finally brought up his concern and provided me with his opinion of what would be in the best interest of the church. It was not a case of me having to ask him what he wanted me to do for him; he was anxious to let me know his opinion before I even had time to be part of the process

> Leadership is about so much more than exerting one's authority.

with the committees and boards that were elected to make such decisions. The same man approached me several times on various issues during my first year, and each time I assured him that I would pass his concern along to those who were responsible for making the decision. What I didn't know, until many years into my ministry there, was that word had gotten around that he tried to influence me but I would not be swayed. I was told that persons appreciated my leadership and the fact that someone "finally stood up to him."

Leaders need to be aware that there will be attempts to gain favoritism by persons who see themselves in positions of power. When James and John approached Jesus, they were looking for position and authority. It is rather like when a parent looks out the kitchen window and sees two children arguing. Moments later, one of them comes in and asks, "Dad, will you do something for me?" Of course, dad is going to ask, "What do you want me to do for you?" It's dad's way of having the child put the desire into words. James and John were quick to tell Jesus their desire for a seating arrangement that would settle the argument of who was the greatest among them.

By way of contrast, Jesus uses the same question with the blind man, illustrating his leadership skill in teaching the disciples to hear how different the blind man's answer was compared to James and John's. For James and John, the request was all about "me"; for the blind man, it was all about "mercy." In both cases Jesus uses the circumstances to teach them about servant leadership. Church leaders can model servant leadership in the way they respond to those who come exercising their power in an effort to influence decisions.

Leadership is about so much more than exerting one's authority or enjoying the perks that come from position. A servant leader, in the model of Jesus, is always more aware and able to see the needs of those whom he or she leads than the leader's own wants and desires. A servant leader is willing to be interrupted. In fact, he or she may find that ministry often happens in the interruptions, just as a deepening in our discipleship often happens when we stop.

In this passage, the same question elicited two very different responses. How would you respond to Jesus' question "What do you want me to do for you?"

Questions for Group Discussion or Personal Reflection
Please read Mark 10:32-52.
1. What does the question that James and John asked suggest to us about them?
2. What does Jesus' answer tell us about Jesus? What does the response of the other ten disciples tell us about them?
3. What is the role of the crowd in this encounter? When have you experienced a "crowd" response (for better or worse) regarding one of your questions?
4. What to you is most significant about Jesus' response to Bartimaeus? Why?
5. When have you used the same question and received two very different responses?
6. What do *you* want Jesus to do for you? Why?

Notes
1. William Barclay, *The Gospel of Mark*, rev. ed., Daily Study Bible Series (Philadelphia: Westminster Press, 1975), 255.

All leaders have stories that can be told only because they refused to walk away.

4

"Do You Also Wish to Go Away?"

JOHN 6:51-71

SCRIPTURE ENCOUNTER

[51] "I am the living bread that came down from heaven. Whoever eats of this bread will live forever; and the bread that I will give for the life of the world is my flesh." [52] The Jews then disputed among themselves, saying, "How can this man give us his flesh to eat?" [53] So Jesus said to them, "Very truly, I tell you, unless you eat the flesh of the Son of Man and drink his blood, you have no life in you. [54] Those who eat my flesh and drink my blood have eternal life, and I will raise them up on the last day; [55] for my flesh is true food and my blood is true drink. [56] Those who eat my flesh and drink my blood abide in me, and I in them. [57] Just as the living Father sent me, and I live because of the Father, so whoever eats me will live because of me. [58] This is the bread that came down from heaven, not like that which your ancestors ate, and they died. But the one who eats this bread will live forever." [59] He said these things while he was teaching in the synagogue at Capernaum.

[60] When many of his disciples heard it, they said, "This teaching is difficult; who can accept it?" [61] But Jesus, being aware that his disciples were complaining about it, said to them, "Does this offend you? [62] Then what if you were to see the Son of Man

ascending to where he was before? [63] It is the spirit that gives life; the flesh is useless. The words that I have spoken to you are spirit and life. [64] But among you there are some who do not believe." For Jesus knew from the first who were the ones that did not believe, and who was the one that would betray him. [65] And he said, "For this reason I have told you that no one can come to me unless it is granted by the Father."

[66] Because of this many of his disciples turned back and no longer went about with him. [67] So Jesus asked the twelve, "Do you also wish to go away?" [68] Simon Peter answered him, "Lord, to whom can we go? You have the words of eternal life. [69] We have come to believe and know that you are the Holy One of God." [70] Jesus answered them, "Did I not choose you, the twelve? Yet one of you is a devil." [71] He was speaking of Judas son of Simon Iscariot, for he, though one of the twelve, was going to betray him.

RELATING TO THE STORY

Life, leadership, and ministry regularly require that we answer some version of this question that Jesus posed to his disciples: "Do you also wish to go away?" Who among us hasn't been ready to throw in the towel or beg off the committee when the task at hand proved far more difficult and challenging than first thought? Perhaps we've even considered this response to our own discipleship along the way. Living a Christ-following life in our surrounding culture increasingly marks us as different from the majority.

> Life, leadership, and ministry regularly require that we answer this question: Do you also wish to go away?

It's the "grass is always greener" phenomenon. The help-wanted ads can look pretty alluring after the difficult congregational meeting, or a week of twelve-hour days that come back to back to back for pastors and lay leaders alike. Researchers tell us that many clergy will leave the ministry within the first five years of their ordination.[1] Most college graduates today will not retire from the same job or even the same discipline in which they entered the workforce. Some of this is the result of a fast-paced and ever-changing economy, but some is by choice—making the conscious decision to walk away.

THE QUESTION IN CONTEXT

This question that Jesus asked appears only in the Gospel of John. Jesus poses it to the Twelve, who have been with him the better part of three years. It is asked of them after "many of his (other) disciples turned back and no longer followed him" (vv. 66-67).

The wording of these verses reminds us that Jesus attracted a good many persons, in addition to the Twelve, who followed him over a period of time for a variety of reasons. A look at the broader context of John 6 will prove helpful in understanding not only Jesus' question but also the circumstances from which it arises.

John 6 begins with Jesus' miracle of feeding the five thousand. The result of this miraculous feeding has translated into a crowd of followers who are determined to make Jesus their king (v. 15). Their resolve results in the crowd's pursuing Jesus across the lake to Capernaum, where he questions their motive by suggesting that they are merely after something more to eat (v. 26).

Jesus then uses the reference to loaves of bread to speak with the multitude about his identity and his purpose. There is a give and take in the dialogue with the crowd, drawing on their collective ancestral understanding of the exodus provision of manna (bread). But, as is often the case, the people and Jesus are talking past one another. The multitude is looking for a sign, similar to Moses' giving of bread to the people. Jesus corrects their memory, stating it was not Moses but God who provided the manna. Then he gives them more than a sign, saying, "I am the bread of life. Whoever comes to me will never be hungry, and whoever believes in me will never be thirsty" (v. 35).

It's a defining moment in which those who are astute know they are no longer having a discourse about literal bread for the stomach. Jesus' words of invitation have caused a stir in the midst of his audience. How can a man, whose parents are known by many in the crowd, claim to have come down as bread from heaven? How can this same man say that he is "living bread" and that those who eat of this bread, which is his flesh, will live forever (v. 51)?

It is here and in the chapters that follow that Jesus begins to lose many of his followers. Like the skin of an onion, they easily peel off and fall away. The previous sign of multiplying loaves and fishes was one thing; the talk of consuming flesh and blood is quite another.

But we must be careful not to hear these words exclusively from our own context and cultural bias. When asked how Jesus' listeners would find his language of "eating flesh and drinking blood," many of us today might respond "gross" or "strange." In fact, for the first-century religious person, brought up in a tradition of ritual sacrifice, such reference would not have been all that unfamiliar. A portion of the animal sacrifice (its flesh) was given to the priests, but other worshipers also received a portion. Jesus' statement is perhaps best understood as hyperbole meant to scandalize. Jesus was trying to shake those who followed him out of their preconceptions.[2] Those who came from mystery religions knew the tradition of eating meat that had been sacrificed to a god, and the tradition that said once the animal flesh was offered, the god entered the flesh. To eat the meat, then, was to actually ingest the god who inhabited it (see 1 Corinthians 8).

Jesus was a master at taking something familiar and giving it new understanding and definition. John's Gospel emphasizes this teaching, in part, to counter heretical doctrine that wanted to deny the physical human body of our Lord. In a general sense, Jesus' flesh represents his complete humanity. In a faith sense, the invitation to eat his flesh and drink his blood was and is an invitation to take his very life into the core of our being. When we eat the bread and drink the blood, we ingest—that is, we take into our very self—our commitment to follow Jesus. We are "all in" with him.

Consider the following illustration. Suppose you have a book on your bookshelf at home or workplace, sitting among several other books. This book is filled with information, but no matter how good and helpful or important that information might be, it takes on meaning only when you take the book down from the shelf and read it. Then the content of the book can be internalized, and in the process of doing so it becomes part of the reader.

But let's take it a step further. Suppose this book is on diet and fitness and contains a plan by which a person can reach an ideal weight and develop a fitness routine to maintain a healthy lifestyle. The information provides practical steps to take toward the pursuit of that goal, but in order to be successful, the person must act on those steps and put that information into practice.

In a similar vein, we might hear Jesus' words as that invitation to action, to take him into our lives, indeed our very selves, and to put his ways into practice. This is a call to discipleship, which moves beyond what Jesus can do for us and centers us in a relationship with the living Christ whereby we are "all in" as those who follow and participate fully in his mission.

All of this—what many in the crowd call a "hard teaching" (v. 60)—leads to the offense and falling away of many of his disciples. This wasn't turning out like they had anticipated. Jesus had raised the expectation of what it would mean to follow him. And many were scandalized by this, and upon watching the many walk away, Jesus turned to the Twelve with his question: "Do you also wish to go away?"

Simon Peter (as usual) speaks for the group. How do you hear his reply in verse 68? "Lord, to whom can we go? You have the words of eternal life. We have come to believe and know that you are the Holy One of God."

Is Peter's answer pessimistic or hopeful? Is he acknowledging, in resigned despair, that there is no turning back now because there is simply no better option? Or, is Peter "all in"? We think it's the latter. In John's Gospel, these words of Simon Peter's are the equivalent of his great confession found in the Synoptic Gospels (see Matthew 16:13-20; Mark 8:27-30; Luke 9:18-21). Do you remember the question that had surfaced among Jesus and the disciples on that occasion? "Who do people say that I am?" After some word-on-the-street answers—"John the Baptist, Elijah, Jeremiah, one of the prophets"—Jesus asked, "What about you? Who do you say that I am?" Then, much like here in John 6, Peter had one of his greatest moments: "You are the Christ, the Son of the living God" or "We believe and know that you are the Holy One of God."

Peter may not have understood everything that Jesus intended for him to understand at this point, but he was committed and loyal to Jesus. He believed he was ready, in that moment, to eat the bread (flesh) and drink the cup (blood) that was being offered.

IMPLICATIONS FOR LIFE AND LEADERSHIP

The implications of Jesus' question and this passage for life and leadership are several. Leading provides continual opportunities to be "all in." Those whom we lead are often watching to ascertain our level of commitment.

Both of us, Dan and Bill, live and serve in the city of Columbus, Indiana. In the summer of 2008, our community was hit by a flash flood. More than ten inches of rain fell a few miles to our north in just a few hours, far exceeding the earth's capacity to absorb that amount of precipitation.

Rivers, creeks, and tributaries soon swelled and sent the water south. By the time the runoff gathered and hit the city of Columbus, the waterways that run through and around our community could not begin to contain the volume of water. A major, one-hundred-year flood enveloped a city of more than forty thousand persons. Individuals were displaced from their homes. Businesses were flooded. The Columbus Regional Hospital was flooded, evacuated, and shut down. Travelers were stranded on one side of the water or another, many with no way to get home and check on their property. In the end, hundreds of homes were rendered uninhabitable. All of this was happening on a Saturday afternoon that, after the rain, turned into a beautiful, sunny day.

> Those whom we lead are often watching to ascertain our level of commitment.

By Sunday, our congregation began to mobilize, checking on individuals and families, learning whom the flood had hit, and making sure all were safe. On Monday morning, volunteers met in our church parking lot, as they would for the next several weeks, to go out into the community and help muck out the homes and businesses of church members, neighbors, and complete strangers who had been most severely impacted.

In many ways, the response of the congregation to the flood was a turning point in how we began to understand our involvement in local missional expressions of ministry. For the pastor, Dan, who had been with the church just six months when the flood hit, this was a turning point of leadership. Word soon spread that Pastor Dan was reporting to work with the volunteer crews, mucking out basements and emerging from crawl spaces covered in the flood's debris. Such moments, and our response to them, are often critical junctures in leadership. A part of us might wish to go away, or wish the crisis would go away, but demonstration of being an all-in leader will be noticed. Can you think of a time when you, as a leader, were determined to be "all in" like this? What was the outcome?

We must embody whatever leadership theory we subscribe to, or else it will remain only a theory. Do you consider yourself a "servant leader"? Then you had best be serving others. Do you warm to the notion of "collaborative leadership"? Then you must demonstrate the ability to work collaboratively with others. When Jesus asked his disciples, "Do you also wish to go away?" he was raising a leadership question as well as a question of discipleship. Were the Twelve ready to lead in his example and likeness? Would they become Christlike as leaders?

> **Questions of discipleship are also often about leadership.**

This hard question, to which several in the crowd took offense, reminds us that leadership today often comes with the potential for the leader to be offended. Perhaps you've been told, as we have, that "it's nothing personal" when someone rejected your offer of assistance or message of help. This happens to church leaders all the time, often as congregants stray or discontinue their former patterns of participation. As excuses are offered, often to pastors, they come with the disclaimer "It's nothing personal." Why is it that it always feels personal?

Consider Bill's story of calling on Jack and Mary, an inactive couple in the first church he pastored. This couple had been active for a couple of years and then stopped coming to Sunday school. Soon they stopped coming to worship. They refused to accept any position of leadership in the church. Aware of this new pattern, Bill called them and made an appointment to sit down and discuss their recent relationship to the church.

They confessed they had done some thinking and concluded that they had been coming to church for the wrong reasons. They had been coming because they wanted to be sure their kids were in Sunday school. They attended regularly because it was important for their children to see them also attend. Now that their last child was off to college, they woke up on Sunday and said, "We don't have to go!" So they went back to sleep. They said they were going to have to be honest about why they would come back, if they would come back. They were considering Jesus' question and the answer was this: "We are leaving because we've been coming for the kids and not for ourselves."

Weeks passed, and finally one Sunday morning, there were Jack and Mary again, sitting in their familiar pew. A few weeks later, they were back in Sunday school and once again willing to accept positions of responsibility in the church. But now it was for the right reasons. They had wanted to respond to Jesus' question personally, and their answer was a decision of renewal and rededication of their discipleship.

We wish that all such stories turned out with such a happy ending. Sadly, they do not. In a day of consumer-driven approaches to faith and church, we will continue to see too many Jacks and Marys fall away. When this happens, we could choose to be offended. We might even write them off or allow the impact of such patterns to drive us to pessimism. Or we might, like Peter, choose to be hopeful, to be "all in" with Jesus and ready to welcome others who answer likewise.

What's your response to Jesus' question "Do you also wish to go away?"

Questions for Group Discussion or Personal Reflection
Please read John 6:51-71.
1. If you were one of the disciples, would you have been offended by Jesus' words about "eating flesh" and "drinking blood"? Why or why not?

2. Have you ever had the thought of giving up on the church but chose not to? What circumstances shaped that thought?
3. Have you ever had a time when you, as a leader, wanted to give up, but didn't? What was the outcome of your decision?
4. How does Jesus' question challenge your discipleship? Your leadership?
5. How do you respond to Jesus' question "Do you also want to go away?" Where in our lives is Christ seemingly offending us by asking for a greater commitment?

Notes

1. Though the research varies by denomination, there is widespread concern for clergy attrition. J.R. Lowell reported in 2010 that among active clergy in the Church of the Nazarene "39.8% have considered leaving active vocational ministry in the past three years." Lowell, Jeren R., "Ministerial Attrition: When Clergy Call It Quits," 2010. http://nazarene.org/files/docs/RelationshipSuperintendentsPastors.pdf.

2. John J. Parsons, "The Life Is in the Blood: New Life and the Greater Exodus," Hebrew for Christians, http://hebrew4christians.com/Articles/Life_in_the_Blood/life_in_the_blood.html.

True leadership values submission for the group's greater good over the achievement of predetermined personal outcomes.

"Are You Still Sleeping and Resting?"

MATTHEW 26:36-56

SCRIPTURE ENCOUNTER

[36] Then Jesus went with them to a place called Gethsemane; and he said to his disciples, "Sit here while I go over there and pray." [37] He took with him Peter and the two sons of Zebedee, and began to be grieved and agitated. [38] Then he said to them, "I am deeply grieved, even to death; remain here, and stay awake with me." [39] And going a little farther, he threw himself on the ground and prayed, "My Father, if it is possible, let this cup pass from me; yet not what I want but what you want." [40] Then he came to the disciples and found them sleeping; and he said to Peter, "So, could you not stay awake with me one hour? [41] Stay awake and pray that you may not come into the time of trial; the spirit indeed is willing, but the flesh is weak." [42] Again he went away for the second time and prayed, "My Father, if this cannot pass unless I drink it, your will be done." [43] Again he came and found them sleeping, for their eyes were heavy. [44] So leaving them again, he went away and prayed for the third time, saying the same words. [45] Then he came to the disciples and said to them, "Are you still sleeping and taking your rest? See, the hour is at hand, and the Son of Man is betrayed into the hands of sinners. [46] Get up, let us be going. See, my betrayer is at hand."

⁴⁷ While he was still speaking, Judas, one of the twelve, arrived; with him was a large crowd with swords and clubs, from the chief priests and the elders of the people. ⁴⁸ Now the betrayer had given them a sign, saying, "The one I will kiss is the man; arrest him." ⁴⁹ At once he came up to Jesus and said, "Greetings, Rabbi!" and kissed him. ⁵⁰ Jesus said to him, "Friend, do what you are here to do." Then they came and laid hands on Jesus and arrested him. ⁵¹ Suddenly, one of those with Jesus put his hand on his sword, drew it, and struck the slave of the high priest, cutting off his ear. ⁵² Then Jesus said to him, "Put your sword back into its place; for all who take the sword will perish by the sword. ⁵³ Do you think that I cannot appeal to my Father, and he will at once send me more than twelve legions of angels? ⁵⁴ But how then would the scriptures be fulfilled, which say it must happen in this way?" ⁵⁵ At that hour Jesus said to the crowds, "Have you come out with swords and clubs to arrest me as though I were a bandit? Day after day I sat in the temple teaching, and you did not arrest me. ⁵⁶ But all this has taken place, so that the scriptures of the prophets may be fulfilled." Then all the disciples deserted him and fled.

RELATING TO THE STORY

Do you have a place of retreat that you frequent or where you make pilgrimage to in your own life? For many in our denomination (American Baptist Churches USA), including the two of us, the Green Lake Conference Center in Green Lake, Wisconsin, has filled such a role. It is holy ground on which generations of leaders and followers have strengthened their faith.

Do you have a place of retreat?

Jesus had Gethsemane, a particular garden where he and the disciples apparently went on a regular basis, and his access to such a retreat probably speaks to the many connections Jesus seems to have cultivated in his ministry. The use of the space speaks to his self-awareness and attention to spiritual and community practices. In the garden, he engaged with God in deep and moving prayer. In the garden, he sought out the support and companionship of his closest friends.

THE QUESTION IN CONTEXT

The garden of Gethsemane sits outside the city of Jerusalem amidst a grove of olive trees. It's a quiet place—a place of retreat. The location outside the city walls was a sanitation requirement of its day, as spreading manure, a common practice in fertilizing gardens, wasn't allowed within the city. In this case, the precaution of cleanliness provided a derivative of separation and what, for Jesus and his disciples, would become sacred space.

The visit to Gethsemane on this night, of course, comes in the midst of trouble. This is the night Jesus would be betrayed, arrested, and rushed to trial. When you face this kind of life-threatening trouble, you do not want to be alone. Even as you engage in the self-work of personal prayer, knowing that there is a small group of friends nearby gives solace in the loneliness of the circumstance. Better yet is if those friends know you well enough to simply be present and not overbearing. It's not Job's chatty friends you need at Gethsemane, but friends who will watch and pray.

When I (Bill) was serving as a hospice chaplain, it was my privilege to journey with individuals and families who were in the valley of the shadow. During those years, I observed how some family and friends were caring and supportive, while others were not sensitive to the needs of the one who was dying.

At 7:00 a.m. one day in our inpatient facility, I approached the room of Irene, a woman who had asked me to visit each morning and read Scripture and pray with her. The door was closed, and there was a sign on the door: "NO VISITORS (check with the nurse's station)." I hadn't heard any report about this in the morning staff review of patients, so I went to the nurse's station and inquired about the reason for the sign and if it included me as a chaplain. The nurse assured me it was not intended for any staff members, but only the family. The nurse also indicated that there was the name of one friend on the list who was permitted to visit.

I entered the room and pulled my chair beside Irene's bed and sat down. Her eyes were closed, so I put my hand softly on top of her hand. She opened her eyes and smiled. "I've been waiting for you," she said.

I inquired how her night's rest was, and she said she had a good night's rest. I asked her, as I did each morning, what portion of the Scriptures she would like me to read. She chose the book of Psalms. I gave her the opportunity to choose any of the psalms, and she said, "Read whichever ones you want, but conclude with Psalm 23."

I read for her, and then I finished with the reading of Psalm 23. After a few moments of silence, I asked her why she requested Psalm 23.

She responded, "It's peaceful and comforting. I need that. Will you pray for me to be able to have this peace? My time is short."

I held her hand and offered a prayer for her, and before I left I asked if she would mind telling me why she asked for a "NO VISITORS" sign to be put on the door.

She said, "As you know, my family is only two nieces who come to visit me. I know they mean well, but while they are here they want the TV on, and they only talk about things that are not at all important to me. They make such a fuss over nothing and argue with each other about silly stuff. It makes me so nervous and restless. I'd rather they not come. I know I may hurt their feelings, but I just can't handle it."

I affirmed her decision, but then I asked, "Who is the person whose name is on the list that you've given permission to see you, and what is so special about her?"

Through her dried parched lips she gave me a big smile and said, "Oh, that's Gracie. She's my best friend. She comes every day and brings her book to read and her Bible. She pulls that easy chair over here next to my bed and sits with me. She tells me if I want to talk, she'll listen, and if I want to sleep, she'll read. All afternoon she sits there. I talk a little and fall asleep. When I wake up, she's right there. She doesn't do anything, but she's with me."

> She doesn't do anything, but she's with me.

If there's one thing we all need when we experience our own Gethsemane, it is the assurance that we are not alone and that someone is with us. Gracie's presence and the promises of Psalm 23 provided Irene with the peace and comfort she needed. Jesus sought that same comfort and companionship from his friends at Gethsemane.

Luke reminds us that since his childhood, Jesus had grown in the framework of wholeness in human development (see Luke 2:52). This framework is built around four parts (intellectual, physical, spiritual, and social-relational) that make up the whole. All four of those parts of Jesus' self were under attack on that night. So he withdrew to Gethsemane, where he sought God and the fellowship of his friends for strength.

But his friends could not stay awake! Why not? How could they sleep? Isn't that the shorthand version of Jesus' question: "Are you still sleeping and resting?"

It's hard not to read disappointment into that question. We can imagine Jesus' tone of voice or expression of exasperation. But a Scripture passage that so readily reveals the humanity of Jesus ought not deny his disciples that same humanity. Sleep comes when we are physically exhausted. Sleep may also be a retreat or escape when we are mentally stressed, spiritually overwhelmed, and relationally taxed. One can almost feel the fatigue of this group of disciples who have been with Jesus through the heavy conversational focus of the Last Supper. Topics of betrayal, as well as Jesus' body and blood, have permeated the evening. And now, a late-night prayer vigil in a quiet garden found even those closest to Jesus fighting and yielding to sleep.

In between checking in on Peter and the two sons of Zebedee, Jesus carried on a prayerful conversation with God (see vv. 39,42,44). What, exactly, was he asking in this prayer? Two things seem likely: verification and the will to submit. Jesus sought to verify that this "cup" (plan for his life) was the one he was to drink (follow or yield to). He sought to know if there was any other way than this way. Was there any other way than his death? Any other way he had overlooked? Was this the way? Should he submit to this way?

From Gethsemane one can look across the Kidron Valley to the place where Abraham went to the mountain to offer up his son Isaac (see Genesis 22). In that experience, God provided another way for Abraham (v. 13). Jesus knew this story. It gives us reason to ponder whether Jesus was remembering it when he asked God if the cup might pass from him. Was there a "ram in the thicket," or was he to be the Lamb of God?

The answer seemed to come to Jesus in stages—or at least the understanding was revealed and accepted over the course of these three intense experiences of prayer. Notice that they were broken up by the appeals and questions to the three disciples: "Could you not keep watch with me for one hour?" (v. 40).

IMPLICATIONS FOR LIFE AND LEADERSHIP

Could it be that Jesus' experience at Gethsemane reveals that while faith is lived in community and experienced in the context of the group (church), it also remains very personal? You alone, just as Jesus alone, can submit to God's will for your life. You can, and should, do it with the support of others, but the decision and act of submission are individual. Discipleship always has these two components at work: individual choice and community nurture and support.

Leadership also involves submission. A true leader submits to the greater goal or greater good rather than force or pursue personal wishes or predetermined outcomes at the group's expense.

> Leadership also involves submission.

Jesus' leadership was willing to lay down his life for his friends, even if they couldn't stay awake with him through the night. When have you practiced submission as a leader?

As a young pastor in ministry, I (Dan) can remember learning the importance of submission in leadership. My zeal to produce results often caused me to bring new ideas to the church boards and committees with which I worked. Much of the time these ideas were endorsed, or at least not verbally denied, by the various ministry groups. This meant that I pursued the ideas with the assumption that board and committee members would exhibit their full support, ownership, and participation. This, however, was not always true. What I discovered was that the ministry group simply did not know how to tell me no, and I was probably projecting an attitude that I would not take no for an answer.

Experience will teach you as a leader that true leadership means working with others who are following and collaborating, not by functioning as a lone ranger who tries to do everything yourself. That type of leadership only yields resentment. Both the church ministry groups and I learned that it was better for them to say, "No" or "Not yet," and for me to submit to their discernment than for us to continue as independent agents. Submission in leadership can be a very good thing to practice.

Jesus' Betrayal and Arrest

Any treatment of the Matthew 26 passage (especially vv. 47-56) must consider the role that Judas plays at Gethsemane. He is the betrayer, but why? Why did Judas do what he did?

One common theory is that Judas was simply trying to kick-start Jesus into leading a rebellion and bringing in a new kingdom. He, like the other disciples, had misunderstood Jesus' teaching on the kingdom of God and believed that it was to be an earthly kingdom—overthrowing the oppression of Rome. And, as the only one of the Twelve not from Galilee, Judas, a Judean, presumably had local connections among the religious community who would be open to his act of intervention and betrayal.

It may be, however, that Judas was somewhat uncertain about his actions as they unfolded. Clues are found in the language used around the word *kiss*. The first Greek word used for "kiss" (v. 48) carries the meaning of a formal Eastern greeting given at the point of meeting. Judas's kiss of greeting was to be the signal identifying Jesus in the darkness of the garden. But in his commentary on the parallel text in Mark 14:44-45, William Barclay observed that the second word used for "kiss" (v. 49; Mark 14:45) is an intensive form, carrying a more intimate connotation of friendship or love.[1] Could this signal that Judas had misgivings about his actions even as he undertook them? Did he realize in the moment that the plan he had devised to spur Jesus to action was about to unfold in a very different direction? It's an interesting point to ponder.

The identified leadership issue at play in Judas's overall behavior is called "transference." He had transferred onto Jesus his own hopes and desires for a messiah who would bring forth the kingdom according to Judas's expectations. His transferred hopes had gone so far as to compel him into the action of betrayal.

Leaders face the issue of transference in congregational life quite often. Many church members expect the leader to mirror their own understandings of leadership and action for the church or ministry. Such expectations often betray their own desires for control and leadership. It's probable that some of this dynamic was at play in Judas's behavior: Jesus was not living up to Judas's expectation of messianic leadership.

So who was truly in charge in the garden? Who demonstrated leadership? To whom did the group defer as leader? The paradox of the story is that Jesus still appears to be the one in charge. Jesus, the object of Judas's betrayal and the one among them for whom an arrest warrant had been issued, took up the leader's mantle. Jesus led through the prayer vigil with the sleepy disciples. He led through the mob scene with the arriving crowd, during which swords were drawn and an ear was sliced. It was Jesus who remained calm and composed and in charge. He stayed awake. He kept watch, even at Gethsemane.

Questions for Group Discussion or Personal Reflection

Please read Matthew 26:36-56.

1. How would you describe Jesus' emotions and what he might have been feeling as he entered the garden of Gethsemane? What do you think the disciples were feeling?

2. In what ways can you identify with the prayer request Jesus made to God? When have you prayed a similar prayer? What was your concern?

3. How might Jesus' question "Are you still sleeping and resting?" be applied to your life of discipleship?

4. What question would you like to ask Judas regarding his role in this Gethsemane story? Why?

5. What's the most important "take-away lesson" for you from this Gethsemane story?

Notes

1. William Barclay, *The Gospel of Mark*, rev. ed., Daily Study Bible Series (Philadelphia: Westminster Press, 1975), 345–46.

*If "faith is the assurance of
things hoped for, the conviction of
things not seen" (Hebrews 11:1),
leadership is helping others step
forward by faith.*

"Do You Believe This?"

JOHN 11:1-53

SCRIPTURE ENCOUNTER

[1] Now a certain man was ill, Lazarus of Bethany, the village of Mary and her sister Martha. [2] Mary was the one who anointed the Lord with perfume and wiped his feet with her hair; her brother Lazarus was ill. [3] So the sisters sent a message to Jesus, "Lord, he whom you love is ill." [4] But when Jesus heard it, he said, "This illness does not lead to death; rather it is for God's glory, so that the Son of God may be glorified through it." [5] Accordingly, though Jesus loved Martha and her sister and Lazarus, [6] after having heard that Lazarus was ill, he stayed two days longer in the place where he was.

[7] Then after this he said to the disciples, "Let us go to Judea again." [8] The disciples said to him, "Rabbi, the Jews were just now trying to stone you, and are you going there again?" [9] Jesus answered, "Are there not twelve hours of daylight? Those who walk during the day do not stumble, because they see the light of this world. [10] But those who walk at night stumble, because the light is not in them." [11] After saying this, he told them, "Our friend Lazarus has fallen asleep, but I am going there to awaken him." [12] The disciples said to him, "Lord, if he has fallen asleep, he will be all right." [13] Jesus, however, had been speaking about his

death, but they thought that he was referring merely to sleep. [14] Then Jesus told them plainly, "Lazarus is dead. [15] For your sake I am glad I was not there, so that you may believe. But let us go to him." [16] Thomas, who was called the Twin, said to his fellow disciples, "Let us also go, that we may die with him."

[17] When Jesus arrived, he found that Lazarus had already been in the tomb four days. [18] Now Bethany was near Jerusalem, some two miles away, [19] and many of the Jews had come to Martha and Mary to console them about their brother. [20] When Martha heard that Jesus was coming, she went and met him, while Mary stayed at home. [21] Martha said to Jesus, "Lord, if you had been here, my brother would not have died. [22] But even now I know that God will give you whatever you ask of him." [23] Jesus said to her, "Your brother will rise again." [24] Martha said to him, "I know that he will rise again in the resurrection on the last day." [25] Jesus said to her, "I am the resurrection and the life. Those who believe in me, even though they die, will live, [26] and everyone who lives and believes in me will never die. Do you believe this?" [27] She said to him, "Yes, Lord, I believe that you are the Messiah, the Son of God, the one coming into the world."

[28] When she had said this, she went back and called her sister Mary, and told her privately, "The Teacher is here and is calling for you." [29] And when she heard it, she got up quickly and went to him. [30] Now Jesus had not yet come to the village, but was still at the place where Martha had met him. [31] The Jews who were with her in the house, consoling her, saw Mary get up quickly and go out. They followed her because they thought that she was going to the tomb to weep there. [32] When Mary came where Jesus was and saw him, she knelt at his feet and said to him, "Lord, if you had been here, my brother would not have died." [33] When Jesus saw her weeping, and the Jews who came with her also weeping, he was greatly disturbed in spirit and deeply moved. [34] He said, "Where have you laid him?" They said to him, "Lord, come and see." [35] Jesus began to weep. [36] So the Jews said, "See how he loved him!" [37] But some of them said, "Could not he who opened the eyes of the blind man have kept this man from dying?"

[38] Then Jesus, again greatly disturbed, came to the tomb. It was a cave, and a stone was lying against it. [39] Jesus said, "Take away the stone." Martha, the sister of the dead man, said to him, "Lord, already there is a stench because he has been dead four days." [40] Jesus said to her, "Did I not tell you that if you believed, you would see the glory of God?" [41] So they took away the stone. And Jesus looked upward and said, "Father, I thank you for having heard me. [42] I knew that you always hear me, but I have said this for the sake of the crowd standing here, so that they may believe that you sent me." [43] When he had said this, he cried with a loud voice, "Lazarus, come out!" [44] The dead man came out, his hands and feet bound with strips of cloth, and his face wrapped in a cloth. Jesus said to them, "Unbind him, and let him go."

[45] Many of the Jews therefore, who had come with Mary and had seen what Jesus did, believed in him. [46] But some of them went to the Pharisees and told them what he had done. [47] So the chief priests and the Pharisees called a meeting of the council, and said, "What are we to do? This man is performing many signs. [48] If we let him go on like this, everyone will believe in him, and the Romans will come and destroy both our holy place and our nation." [49] But one of them, Caiaphas, who was high priest that year, said to them, "You know nothing at all! [50] You do not understand that it is better for you to have one man die for the people than to have the whole nation destroyed." [51] He did not say this on his own, but being high priest that year he prophesied that Jesus was about to die for the nation, [52] and not for the nation only, but to gather into one the dispersed children of God. [53] So from that day on they planned to put him to death.

RELATING TO THE STORY

It is a question of simple form but great depth. Just four words: "Do you believe this?" At first glance, it seems to call for validation or agreement and little more. But we have come to see Jesus' use of this simply phrased question in John 11 as profound for the depth and reflection that it calls for in its recipients—then and now.

"Do you believe this?" as it is used in the eleventh chapter of the Fourth Gospel is a question of both discipleship and leadership. It may take exploration beyond the surface of the passage in order to convince you of this. But if you will set aside, for a moment, the miraculous nature of the story that we've come to know as "the raising of Lazarus," you will be released to glean many insights through the dialogue that transpires between Lazarus's sisters and Jesus.

When someone asks, "Do you believe this?" that person is introducing the threads that make the fabric of discipleship possible—things such as faith, hope, commitment, and belief. But these threads are present in the midst of their very opposite elements of understanding. Darker threads of suspicion and hostility, doubt and disbelief, are here as well. Their presence is acknowledged by this same question.

"Do you believe this?" is a question that forces a choice. It is not friendly toward fence sitting or neutrality. Jesus wanted Martha to wrestle with what she believed to be true. With which set of beliefs (which threads) would she move forward: the positive or the negative? Jesus wanted Mary to confront her own beliefs, and, through the very same question, we are asked to name what we believe to be true.

> "Do you believe this?" is a question that forces a choice.

"Do you believe this?" is a question that resurfaces over a lifetime of following Christ. Again and again the question comes to us: "Do I believe this?" about my faith, as a result of my faith. It comes to us in the high moments of celebration and victory, but even more so in the lower moments of doubt, discouragement, and dead ends. It's in answering the question that we move forward and, one might say, deeper in faith and discipleship.

As leaders, we are confronted by Jesus' question in additional ways. Do we believe in the direction, values, and mission that we are leading others to follow as we follow Christ together? Do we believe, in the face of obstacles and improbability, that a resurrection-like result is possible when the immediate evidence may say otherwise? There is much to explore with Jesus' question in John 11.

THE QUESTION IN CONTEXT

Jesus enjoyed a special friendship with the family of Martha, Mary, and Lazarus. Their home, located just a couple of miles from Jerusalem in the village of Bethany, may have served as a place of retreat and rest for Jesus and his disciples on more than one occasion (see Luke 10:38-42). It's interesting that John identifies the setting as "the village of Mary and her sister Martha" and not as the home of Lazarus. This may indicate the sisters' prominence and notoriety within the community, and perhaps also the possibility that Lazarus is their younger brother.

In the Fourth Gospel, Mary is further identified as the one who anointed Jesus' feet with perfume (John 12:1-8). And, in the message sent to Jesus regarding his illness, Lazarus is described as "he whom you love" (John 11:3). Each of these references appears to reinforce the preexisting relationship between Jesus and the family. They set the stage for Jesus' unexpected response to the news that Lazarus was ill.

When the sisters dispatched the message concerning their brother's illness to Jesus, the message was apparently sent with the certainty that Jesus would drop what he was doing and come to their aid. There was a good deal of confusion, not only in Bethany but also among the disciples, in how Jesus responded to the message. His delay in going to Bethany—"he stayed two days longer in the place where he was" (v. 6)—is variously interpreted. The disciples seemed to think that Jesus meant that Lazarus's illness was not very serious, and that if he was only sleeping (v. 12), he would soon be fully recovered. In contrast, Martha and Mary were perplexed by Jesus' delayed arrival, as indicated by their common refrain: "Lord, if you had been here, my brother would not have died" (vv. 21,32).

It was Jesus who set his disciples straight with the news that "Lazarus is dead" (v. 14), indicating that he had knowledge all along of the seriousness of the situation. But Jesus' unique insight into the circumstances and gravity of Lazarus's illness did little to clear up the confusion for the others. Why would Jesus have intentionally delayed responding to the appeal of his friends? It seems so out of character for him not to go and show immediate compassion. So, as the disciples worried about his safety (v. 8), misunderstood his references to light and darkness (life and death) (vv. 9-10), and through Thomas's voice pronounced their allegiance with him unto death (v. 16), Jesus finally did move the delegation to Bethany, knowing something that the others did not as yet know.

IMPLICATIONS FOR LIFE AND LEADERSHIP

Often a leader does know or see something that others do not. Sometimes this knowledge or insight is because another has trusted and shared information with the leader. At other times it is because of the leader's experience, intuition, or read of the situation. Of course, pastoral leaders often operate in the realm of confidential knowledge when it comes to pastoral care and counseling. And in congregational systems, leaders often have advance knowledge and more information going into a situation that, ultimately, they are trying to lead others through.

The leadership determination is what to do, or not do, with the knowledge you have. A leader who has no filters when it comes to revealing knowledge or information may be far less effective than one who operates with a sense of discernment, wisdom, and timing on when, to whom, and how information is best shared. We see evidence of this in Jesus' behavior with the disciples and Lazarus's family at Bethany.

Jesus operates among them with both knowledge and a great sense of timing and purpose. He has a bigger picture in mind. He is able to lead all who are involved toward the destination of his mission among them.

I (Bill) relate to Jesus' decision as it concerns leadership knowledge. Once, when I had just arrived at a vacation destination, I received a telephone call from a person in the church where I was serving as senior pastor. She said that there had been a death, and it was important for me to return for the funeral. She explained the circumstances and the importance this family played in the life and history of the church. I asked her if she would give me a few minutes, and I would get right back to her. She agreed. I immediately called one of my associates, the only other pastoral staff person available. He was a young associate only two years out of seminary. His first year with the former senior pastor had been a disaster because he had received no guidance and mentoring from him. When we began working together, I heard his cry for mentoring, and I had provided that over the past year. Both of my associates were involved in all pastoral duties with shut-ins and hospital visits and funerals, so he had some training, and I had confidence in him. I asked him if he would be willing to handle the details of pastoral care for the family and the funeral. He needed assurance that he could do it, and I agreed that he could call me and review any of his preparations. I told him it would be a convincing demonstration of how he was growing in his position.

> Often a leader does know or see something that others do not.

When I called the woman back and shared my decision, she was startled that I would think he would be able to do the kind of job that was expected of their pastors. "He doesn't have any experience," she said. I told her that was my decision, and I was willing to take that chance.

I called the associate back and told him how important this was both for him and for me. Since I had been at the church only eighteen months, I knew I was taking a risk, but I also had seen tremendous growth in the associate and knew he needed this chance to prove himself publicly to the congregation.

After the service he called me and said he felt good about how everything went, in every aspect of the details. As soon as I hung up, the woman from the church called me and said, "I just want to let you know that he did an outstanding job. The family was so pleased with the way he handled everything, and the folks at church were surprised that he could do that. I'm sorry I didn't trust your judgment."

Just as Jesus had confidence that his actions were going to be for the good of all concerned, I too was confident that my decision was also going to be for the good of the church and for a young associate, who two years later accepted a call to a lead pastoral position.

Both discipleship and leadership involve asking and inviting questions of discovery to which you as leader know the answers. I (Bill) knew that my colleague would be capable of ministering to a bereaved family in the congregation. Jesus knew the answers to questions that he posed to the disciples and to Mary and Martha. But in posing the question "Do you believe this?" he provided them an opportunity for growth and faith.

The disciples saw only the fear of what others would do to them, while Jesus saw it as an opportunity. The initial reactions of my colleague and my parishioner were ones of uncertainty, while I understood it as an opportunity. When and where have you been given a similar "Do you believe this?" opportunity for growth in faith or leadership?

Something More Than a Quick Fix

When Martha went out to meet Jesus as he finally arrived (v. 20), she appeared to be overcome with grief. There is the ring of disappointment, perhaps even anger, in her words as she suggested that the outcome of death could have been avoided had Jesus responded sooner. As a loving older sister, Martha had been looking for a quick fix to her brother's illness. She had identified Jesus as the one who could provide that fix, and thus she had sent for him to come.

In this respect, Martha is no different than most of us. We are a people and culture of the quick fix. When something is broken, we call in the expert to fix it. We grow frustrated when that fix is delayed or denied—be it a fix for a broken appliance, a serious illness, an underperforming organization, or even a fractured relationship. In the midst of her grief Martha had not completely let go of her desire for Jesus to fix things. She said to him, "But even now I know that God will give you whatever you ask of him" (v. 22).

> **We are a people and culture of the quick fix.**

As a hospice chaplain, Bill often experienced similar responses to grief and loss among the family members of patients. The need to assign blame is strong when a fix doesn't happen and death comes. Statements that begin with "If only I had . . ." or "If only I had not . . ." remind us that we long for answers to our "why" questions and are willing to even blame ourselves in order to find some semblance of closure. But our experiences with grief tell us that quick fixes are not always, perhaps not often, possible.

As a regional judicatory staff member who often resourced pastoral search committees, Dan observed similar yearnings for quick fixes in the congregations and committees that he worked alongside for nearly nine years. As these committees assessed their leadership needs and shared dreams of the future for their congregation, the new pastor was often spoken of in terms of one who would come into the system and fix what was broken. We might call this the "plug and play" mentality of leadership. It operates with a mechanical metaphor: a part breaks down, and we change it out for a new part that we plug in to solve the problem. The part might be the new pastor or the new programs that he or she will introduce. Unfortunately for this mentality (but fortunately for the church), congregations do not operate like machines. They are living organisms that carry with them histories and leadership challenges much more complex than a simple fix can address.

The leadership term for this type of quick-fix thinking is "technical" or "tactical" leadership. It is one of three approaches to leadership identified by Kevin Ford and Ken Tucker in their book *The Leadership Triangle*.[1] These authors estimate that as many as 90 percent of leaders default to a tactical approach.[2] There will always be a place for tactical leadership within organizations, but it will work best only when a straightforward operational problem can be solved by the knowledge or expertise of the one addressing it.

In many cases, the challenges confronting organizations today, including churches, are much more complex and adaptive than tactical in nature. Forcing tactical leadership approaches on these challenges only enhances frustration. Instead, such challenges require what Ford and Tucker call "transformational" leadership—a form of leading that is able to engage the values, behaviors, and attitudes of the organization. Transformational leadership will even provoke conflict over those values "so that clarity can be reached and real change created."[3]

We would argue that whereas Martha was looking for a tactical (quick-fix) approach from Jesus, he offered her a transformational approach. What made Jesus' leadership in this context transformational? He was challenging Martha's core beliefs about life and death, including eternity. By his delay, one could argue, Jesus provoked a situation through which real change could be introduced (Lazarus's resurrection). In his conversation with Martha (vv. 21-27) he began to point her away from technical thinking to transformational thinking. Let's take another look at the dialogue:

Jesus: "Your brother will rise again" (v. 23).
Martha: "I know that he will rise again in the resurrection on the last day" (v. 24).
Jesus: "I am the resurrection and the life. Those who believe in me, even though they die, will live, and everyone who lives and believes in me will never die. Do you believe this?" (vv. 25-26).

Jesus didn't just fix the situation. He asked for Martha's involvement with his question "Do you believe this?" He wasn't just offering her the platitudes of what's expected during grief—resurrection on the last day. He challenged her beliefs and faith in that moment, and he invited her into a transformational way of thinking and acting. She was able to affirm, "Yes, Lord, I believe that you are the Messiah, the Son of God." (v. 27).

In this transformational moment of her discipleship, Martha was coming to own her response to Jesus' question in a very personal way. She was no longer just voicing the expected response of her faith tradition—resurrection on the last day; rather, she was affirming her belief in Jesus' identity as the Messiah. She was opening herself to a transformation experience, one that later would involve her giving permission for Lazarus's tomb to be opened as he was called forth in resurrection. In her grief and emotion Martha did not yet fully comprehend all that Jesus was asking, but in her affirmation of his identity as the Messiah she was able to move forward.

Herein lies one of the applicable truths of this story for our own discipleship. The truth in this exchange for us is that in the midst of our own unfortunate and unwanted life circumstances we too can hold on to the basic belief that Jesus is Lord. This transformational belief may not immediately change the circumstances, but it moves us forward by helping us find the threads of hope, faith, and commitment—some of what Jesus identifies as "light" (v. 9)—in the midst of darkness. The affirmation of Jesus' lordship reframes our perspective and outlook. We can affirm that one more knowledgeable and powerful than I is present, involved, and in control.

A Leader Who Meets Us Where We Are

While Martha had come out to greet Jesus, Mary was back in the house (v. 20). Martha returned from her encounter with Christ and encouraged her sister to go see him as well (v. 28). Had Jesus, in fact, called for Mary? Or was this Martha's way of ensuring that Mary would go and confront Jesus as well? We cannot be certain, but we do know that their reunion was filled with emotion.

Jesus was subjected to the very same statement that he had received earlier from Martha: "Lord, if you had been here, my brother would not have died" (v. 32). The sentiment conveyed in these words, shared verbatim, may have been rehearsed by the two sisters in their conversations in the days subsequent to Jesus' arrival. The accumulation of emotion and its presentation in these sisters whom Jesus loved and in the grief of the gathered community spilled forth in Jesus' own expressions of loss and sorrow. No longer can we hold on to the falsehood that Jesus was uncaring or stoic in the face of Lazarus's illness or death. Jesus grieved. Jesus wept. Jesus was overcome by the sorrow of a life—his friend's life—that had ended. These behaviors are a reminder to us that God grieves death and loss. When we ask, "Where was God in this?" the answer so often is that God was right there with us, suffering alongside us.

> **Jesus met the sisters where they were.**

No two persons respond to loss in quite the same way. Jesus met Mary's sorrow with his own tears. He met Martha's defiance with a faith dialogue and a question: "Do you believe this?" The leadership point that we would identify in each meeting is that Jesus met the sisters where they were. He led from alongside them, in their very midst. He joined them in conversation. He joined them in sorrow. He invited them to follow and he moved forward with them—not detached or way out in front, but in the midst of and alongside. He helped them overcome the paralysis of the situation, their doubts and disappointments, as well as the derision of the crowd (v. 37). Nothing less than transformation awaits.

Two times in this passage we have been told that Lazarus has been dead for four days: in verse 17 and again in Martha's response (v. 39) to Jesus' command to "take away the stone" lying across the tomb. Such repetition points to a detail that is of significance. It establishes that Lazarus was really deceased. According to the cultural traditions of the Jewish rabbis, "the soul hovered near the body for three days but after that there was no hope of resuscitation," and decay would begin.[4]

Jesus reacted to Martha's objections by reminding her of their earlier conversation: "Did I not tell you that if you believed, you would see the glory of God?" (v. 40). Then, in a transformational act that only God could achieve, Jesus called Lazarus forth from the tomb, from death to life. What was dead was alive. What was lost was found. What was hopeless was now filled with hope. What was over had begun anew. What was bound was loosed.

Truly it was a transformational day—certainly for Lazarus, but equally so for his sisters, for the disciples, and for many in the crowd. Would such an outcome have been possible if Jesus had dropped everything upon hearing of Lazarus's illness and come? No. But a leader had knowledge that others did not. He didn't come to fix things or offer a quick, tactical solution. He came to transform things. He came to weave together the threads of hope, faith, and belief in the discipleship of many by asking the question "Do you believe this?"

What's true for our discipleship is also true for our leadership. So many who lead in the church today can benefit from Jesus' question "Do you believe this?" Faced with circumstances for which we have little or no experience or expertise, we too often apply tactical leadership to adaptive challenges. Frustration only mounts as these "quick-fix" approaches to complex and new obstacles end in disappointment. We cannot plug and play our way out of this new day.

> As leaders, we need the transformation of Jesus' words of hope.

We grieve what once was and worry about what will be. We watch congregations and denominations age and decline. We hear the emotion of those whom we love and their frequent, seemingly rehearsed refrains: "This is not the way it used to be." "We're just an older congregation." "Pastor, I don't know what you're going to do about it."

In the everyday work of leading we are often overcome by doubt. Do we believe this? Do we believe we can do this? Maybe, but maybe not. Maybe not today. Not in this moment of struggle. Not after that difficult meeting, or after reading that treasurer's report. Sometimes we who lead have reason to wonder why the Lord tarries. Didn't Jesus get the message? Didn't he hear our plea?

What does Jesus know that we do not know? As leaders, we need the transformation of Jesus' words of hope. We need somebody to ask us what we believe.

Who provides those words? Who asks that question? We provide them to one another, or we should. Aren't we in this together? The fallacy that a leader is always out front and working alone needs to be rejected. Leaders who are among the people, engaged together in the work, are more likely to have support and encouragement when they dare to express doubt. They, like Martha, need to be reminded of what they believe, for it's in the enactment of that belief that transformation is found. Do you believe this?

We are a people of resurrection. We are people of faith. We are people of hope. The raising of Lazarus was the final sign in John's Gospel of Jesus' identity prior to his own death and resurrection. It served to identify Jesus as one who came among the people as the Messiah. From this point on there was no fence sitting with regard to what persons thought of him or his mission. Those who plotted for his death and demise were emboldened by what happened at Bethany (vv. 46-53). But many others (v. 45) believed in him, and for them, life would forever be different. It was forever transformed.

In our opinion, those who predict the demise of the church in its many forms today need to revisit the power of resurrection and the hope of Christ. And those who are discouraged as they lead would do well to revisit Jesus' question.

There's no doubt that things are changing, and that leadership is hard in many ministry contexts today. But we rest our hope in the conviction that the One (Christ) who leads us knows more than we do. We have faith that he has not abandoned us, but instead walks among us and meets us with questions such as this one in John 11. "Do you believe this?"

Questions for Group Discussion or Personal Reflection

Please read John 11:1-53.

1. Which of the biblical characters in this story can you most identify with: Martha, Mary, the disciples, or Jesus? Why?

2. Think of a time when you, as a leader, had knowledge that others did not have. How did you use or share that knowledge? What risks were involved?

3. In what way have you seen your faith community looking for "quick fixes" (tactical solutions) to what may be more complex challenges? How might this story cause you to rethink that approach?

4. When have you experienced the leadership of one who lead from alongside, or in the midst of the group? What was that like?

5. How has the question "Do you believe this?" confronted you as a disciple? As a leader?

Notes

1. Kevin Ford and Ken Tucker, *The Leadership Triangle: The Three Options That Will Make You a Stronger Leader* (New York: Morgan James, 2013). For a brief overview of these three types of leadership, see appendix C.

2. Ibid., 31–32.

3. Ibid., 29.

4. Raymond E. Brown, *The Gospel According to John I-XII: A New Translation with Introduction and Commentary*, Anchor Bible 29 (New York: Doubleday, 1966), 424.

Leadership is often the confluence of one's personal experience, gifts or strengths, and passion or sense of call.

"Do You Love Me More Than These?"

JOHN 21:1-17

SCRIPTURE ENCOUNTER

[1] After these things Jesus showed himself again to the disciples by the Sea of Tiberias; and he showed himself in this way. [2] Gathered there together were Simon Peter, Thomas called the Twin, Nathanael of Cana in Galilee, the sons of Zebedee, and two others of his disciples. [3] Simon Peter said to them, "I am going fishing." They said to him, "We will go with you." They went out and got into the boat, but that night they caught nothing.

[4] Just after daybreak, Jesus stood on the beach; but the disciples did not know that it was Jesus. [5] Jesus said to them, "Children, you have no fish, have you?" They answered him, "No." [6] He said to them, "Cast the net to the right side of the boat, and you will find some." So they cast it, and now they were not able to haul it in because there were so many fish. [7] That disciple whom Jesus loved said to Peter, "It is the Lord!" When Simon Peter heard that it was the Lord, he put on some clothes, for he was naked, and jumped into the sea. [8] But the other disciples came in the boat, dragging the net full of fish, for they were not far from the land, only about a hundred yards off.

[9] When they had gone ashore, they saw a charcoal fire there, with fish on it, and bread. [10] Jesus said to them, "Bring some

of the fish that you have just caught." ¹¹ So Simon Peter went aboard and hauled the net ashore, full of large fish, a hundred fifty-three of them; and though there were so many, the net was not torn. ¹² Jesus said to them, "Come and have breakfast." Now none of the disciples dared to ask him, "Who are you?" because they knew it was the Lord. ¹³ Jesus came and took the bread and gave it to them, and did the same with the fish. ¹⁴ This was now the third time that Jesus appeared to the disciples after he was raised from the dead.

¹⁵ When they had finished breakfast, Jesus said to Simon Peter, "Simon son of John, do you love me more than these?" He said to him, "Yes, Lord; you know that I love you." Jesus said to him, "Feed my lambs." ¹⁶ A second time he said to him, "Simon son of John, do you love me?" He said to him, "Yes, Lord; you know that I love you." Jesus said to him, "Tend my sheep." ¹⁷ He said to him the third time, "Simon son of John, do you love me?" Peter felt hurt because he said to him the third time, "Do you love me?" And he said to him, "Lord, you know everything; you know that I love you." Jesus said to him, "Feed my sheep."

RELATING TO THE STORY

The need for forgiveness and reconciliation are common to life. Each of us can relate to reconciling with a spouse or family member after a disagreement. We may even be able to identify with the restoration or reinstatement of a relationship that had once been broken between friends or vocational colleagues. Living with the tensions of disappointment, distance, and personal offense does little for our health or well-being. We know the inner compulsion to make things right and repair what has become broken.

Surely Simon Peter was feeling some mixture of these things as he encountered the risen Jesus, and especially as their reunion came to a very personal focal point with Jesus' question in John 21: "Do you love me more than these?"

THE QUESTION IN CONTEXT

Let's revisit what has transpired between Jesus and Peter leading up to this moment. At Gethsemane Peter was among those trusted friends who could not stay awake to watch with Jesus during his time of suffering. During Jesus' arrest, Peter struck out with a sword, taking off the ear of the high priest's servant, only to face Jesus' rebuke (John 18:10-11). Earlier Peter had professed his unyielding allegiance to Jesus, even unto death (John 13:37). But during Jesus' trial Peter's denials had come once, twice, three times (John 18:15-27).

If any of the disciples carried an unresolved tension within them, even after having been in the presence of the risen Christ, it must have been Peter. Those early and fleeting appearances of Jesus among the Twelve had been wonderful and miraculous, filled with joy. But, one imagines, there had been little time for personal conversation—and most certainly not the intense focus required for repairing a relationship that was in such need of restoration as Peter's with Jesus. No, that had to wait. It waited until at least the third time Jesus appeared to his disciples (v. 14). And, in the meantime, Peter had returned to what he knew best: fishing.

Should this surprise us? One of the more common behaviors during times of change and unsettledness is to return to what is familiar. Social science identifies this as our need for equilibrium—for everything to be in balance and at rest. We might think of it as a rubber band that has been stretched tight with equal strength at each end. When

> The rubber band snaps back to a place of rest.

one end is released, what happens? The rubber band snaps back to a place of rest.

For three years, and especially for the past week or more, Jesus' disciples had been undergoing the tension of change.

Their lives had been turned on end. Their purpose was redefined. With Jesus' death, and even through the early reports of his resurrection, the system that they had grown accustomed to had been radically altered. It's natural that they would revert back to old behaviors and practices. For Peter that meant fishing—a familiar, comfortable routine of life on which he could depend. "I'm going fishing," Peter said; "We'll go with you," came the reply (v. 3). When your life has been turned on end, what behavior or practices do you return to?

The fact that the others follow Peter to the boat and a night of fishing may suggest that they needed to remain together (whether they were all fishermen or not). It also hints at a recognition within the group that Peter now occupies the role of leader. A transition was afoot. Jesus was not with them in a regular day-to-day way now. Peter was. Groups look for leaders when they lose theirs. Peter, flawed and fractured as he was, resembled the natural heir to the role.

All of this was in the atmosphere on this occasion: a flawed leader in need of rehabilitation, a failed fishing trip that does little to calm their nerves or set things right, and a most unexpected encounter that points them (especially Peter) back on course.

Isn't this the rhythm of discipleship, as well as of interpersonal relationships? Don't we often take two steps forward and one step back as we practice our faith and follow Christ? Doesn't change, most especially the inner change of our hearts and souls, follow a more circuitous than direct route? Might we too have a hard time leaving things behind and need to be asked, "Do you love me more than these?"

What prompted those weary disciples, who had been out all night fishing, to take the advice of a stranger from the beach? Have you ever wondered about that? Were they becoming so used to the unexpected and miraculous in life that they'd become open to what may have seemed to be a silly direction? Was there something in the tone, the voice, or the expression of this stranger that rang familiar? Did they figure they had nothing to lose?

Recognition seems to have been confirmed in the miraculous haul of fish. Things like this, in their recent experience, were associated with Jesus. One calls out, "It's the Lord!" and Simon Peter can wait no longer for his reunion.

Was it here that Peter's restoration began, in that moment as he took this first quick, bold steps and strokes toward Jesus? Isn't it as he cannot contain himself, can no longer be alone with the weight of his feelings and regret, that he now runs and swims to Jesus? He literally throws himself into the water—eager, anxious, ready to be restored.

Too often we limit such decisive actions in our discipleship to our first steps toward Jesus, when in fact these reunion and restoration moments may happen all along our faith journey. Too often we label them the things of conversion and redemption, as though those comprise a one-time event. But following Jesus brings repeated opportunities for growth, restoration, and responsibility. Just ask Simon.

Simon? That's right. Did you notice that in each of three times Jesus asked Peter his question, "Do you love me," he addressed him as "Simon"? "Simon" was Peter's old name, the name he was known by before Jesus called him the "Rock" (*Petros*). In using the old name, was Jesus pointing out that Simon had returned to his old ways? Was he challenging him to answer as Peter, the Rock?

IMPLICATIONS FOR LIFE AND LEADERSHIP

I (Bill) recall the last weekend of my Holy Land visit when our group was led from our hotel down through a path of overgrown shrubs to the beach at Galilee. It was just minutes before sunrise as we exited the shrubbery path and walked in a silent vigil toward the water's edge. As we drew near the shoreline, we discovered the remains of a charcoal fire that had burned itself out. It was Sunday morning, and our group leader, Dr. Omar Barth, was scheduled to lead our worship together. No one spoke, but we all looked at the burned-out charcoal and at one another as the sun began to rise over the Galilean lake. Dr. Barth opened his Bible to this resurrection text in John 21 and read it for us. We stood there imagining how those disciples pulled in the full net of fish while Jesus tended the fire preparing them breakfast. I do not have words to describe the feelings I had identifying with those disciples, and especially Peter, as the question was asked of us, "Do you love me more than these?" It was this sunrise experience that was the highlight of my three-week visit. I can only imagine that Peter never forgot it either.

What about that question itself: "Do you love me more than these?" What is the "these" to which Jesus refers? Do you love me more than these other guys do? Do you love me more than this way of life? Do you love me more than fishing? Are the 153 fish (v. 11)—a successful catch—the "these"?

One cannot escape the symmetry that this scene offers. Three times Peter had denied having anything to do with Jesus. Three times Jesus asked him this most personal and painful question of restoration. Three times Peter had to answer, pledging his faith to and in Jesus anew. Formation happens in such ways—that is, with repetition. We'd like to think that once is enough, and perhaps sometimes it is, but in order to be truly formed and shaped into something, someone new, repetition is required.

> Practice doesn't make perfect; practice makes permanent.

To borrow from the practice of both music and athletics, we might acknowledge having heard the phrase "practice makes perfect." But a gifted musician at the top of his craft, or an elite athlete who has honed her body into top condition, might suggest otherwise. Practice doesn't make perfect; practice makes permanent. The repetition of practice forms and shapes the response of body, muscle, reaction, thought into ever more permanent patterns.

In similar fashion, practicing our faith brings formation to us as both leaders and disciples. Peter's encounter with Jesus and the need to respond three times to this question began to further shape and form him into the leader he would be for the other disciples and the early church.

Consider another element of symmetry in the story. Jesus' first call of Simon Peter to become his disciple happened on the shores of the Sea of Galilee in the presence of fishing nets, gear, and boat (Matthew 4:18-22). This call of Simon Peter came along that same shore, in the presence of similar fishing equipment. Much had happened in the three years between the call stories. Simon answered the call to discipleship during that first encounter. Peter was answering a call to leadership during this final encounter.

Jesus' question was the tool he used to remind Simon Peter that Jesus had already given him a new identity. No longer would he be Simon, the fisherman from Galilee; now he was the Rock (*Petros*), the leader, the shepherd who was called and commissioned to "feed my sheep."

Can you relate to such a change in identity or role? One of the things that we (Bill and Dan) share in common is a somewhat similar life journey. We are two Midwestern boys from blue-collar, working-class backgrounds, separated in age by about twenty-five years, who each heard God's call to pastoral ministry. Neither of us took up the family business, although there may have been opportunity for both of us to do so. Bill remembers helping his dad in a family painting business after school, on weekends, and during summers. Dan worked for his dad in similar fashion in the family ready-mix concrete and block business.

We both entered our college years with the intent to pursue a degree in education—to teach. But, experiences along the way challenged that intent as God put persons in our path who asked us questions.

For me (Bill), the question came at an unexpected time from a person I had just met, and I was offended. I was in the beginning of my sophomore year at the University of Akron. Our minister of music, who was entertaining a guest missionary from Borneo, invited me out to lunch. It was a free lunch, and what college student turns down such an offer? I still remember the car pulling up to the curb and my getting in the back seat behind where the missionary was sitting in the front. I was introduced to him, and he immediately asked me what class I had just come from. I explained it was a class in teaching the fundamentals of indoor sports. (I was a physical education major.) He asked, "What was the subject today?" I said, "It was a curriculum outlining the fundamentals of teaching students how to play Ping-Pong." He turned and looked over the seat and asked me, "Are you going to spend the rest of your life teaching kids how to play Ping-Pong?"

> God puts persons in our path to ask us questions.

I was offended because I was convinced that I could be a Christian teacher who would have influence upon students. I made a brief comment regarding that as my goal, and there was no further discussion of the matter. But the question haunted me for days. I began wrestling with the idea that God just might have something different for me to do. My struggle lasted several months before I finally received a very clear understanding that God was calling me into Christian ministry. And it all started with an offending question: "Are you going to spend the rest of your life teaching kids how to play Ping-Pong?"

For me (Dan), it wasn't one occasion or question, but the repetition of a question, sometimes voiced and at other times felt: "Have you considered the ministry?" This question was raised by preachers whom I listened to as a young person, by a campus minister who served as a mentor, and by pastors and regional ministers whom I encountered while serving on staff at a summer church camp.

As these persons observed my life and my gifts and engaged me in conversation in my late teens and early twenties, they were bold enough to ask, in some fashion, "Have you considered the ministry?" Truth be told, until I first heard the question, I had not. But with that question repeatedly coming before me, I began to see myself in a different light.

The point is that questions like these led us in a different direction. Ministry became not just a possibility for each of us, but a way of life. And years down the road we found ourselves living in the same community, connected with the same congregation, which we've had the privilege of serving as pastor decades apart.

Christ can change your life with his questions—if you will listen, if you will respond. It may not be change that leads you into vocational ministry. But it may be change that allows you, like Simon Peter (or Bill Griffith or Dan Cash), to see yourself and your life differently.

How might you respond to Jesus' question: "Do you love me more than these?"

Questions for Group Discussion or Personal Reflection

Please read John 21:1-17.

1. How do you relate to Simon Peter's decision to go fishing in Galilee? Does this surprise you? Why? Why not? What statement was made by the other disciples in agreeing to go with him?
2. What do you believe is the focus of this story? Why?
3. What might be the meaning of "these" if Jesus is asking you, "Do you love me more than these?"
4. How do you identify with the process by which Simon Peter's relationship with Jesus is restored?
5. What might Jesus be expecting of you by saying, "Feed . . . tend my sheep"?

The key to successful spiritual leadership has much more to do with the leader's internal life than with the leader's expertise, gifts, or experience.[1]

"What Then Did You Go Out to See?"

LUKE 7:18-30

SCRIPTURE ENCOUNTER

[18] The disciples of John reported all these things to him. So John summoned two of his disciples [19] and sent them to the Lord to ask, "Are you the one who is to come, or are we to wait for another?" [20] When the men had come to him, they said, "John the Baptist has sent us to you to ask, 'Are you the one who is to come, or are we to wait for another?'" [21] Jesus had just then cured many people of diseases, plagues, and evil spirits, and had given sight to many who were blind. [22] And he answered them, "Go and tell John what you have seen and heard: the blind receive their sight, the lame walk, the lepers are cleansed, the deaf hear, the dead are raised, the poor have good news brought to them. [23] And blessed is anyone who takes no offense at me."

[24] When John's messengers had gone, Jesus began to speak to the crowds about John: "What did you go out into the wilderness to look at? A reed shaken by the wind? [25] What then did you go out to see? Someone dressed in soft robes? Look, those who put on fine clothing and live in luxury are in royal palaces. [26] What then did you go out to see? A prophet? Yes, I tell you, and more than a prophet. [27] This is the one about whom it is written,

'See, I am sending my messenger ahead of you,
who will prepare your way before you.'

[28] I tell you, among those born of women no one is greater than John; yet the least in the kingdom of God is greater than he." [29] (And all the people who heard this, including the tax collectors, acknowledged the justice of God, because they had been baptized with John's baptism. [30] But by refusing to be baptized by him, the Pharisees and the lawyers rejected God's purpose for themselves.)

RELATING TO THE STORY

Have you ever answered a question with a question? Somewhere along the way many pastors and church leaders learn this leadership technique. A question surfaces in a Bible study, in a board or ministry team meeting, or in a general conversation. Rather than give an immediate answer, the leader turns another question back to the one making the inquiry. Why do such a thing? Perhaps it is to stall and buy some time to think. More likely it is to invite the person or group raising the initial question to reflect further on their inquiry. The intent is to invite them, based on their observations, to answer their own question.

This is some of the theory behind leadership coaching and discipleship making—that the person being coached, or the disciple being shaped, has within her or himself the ability to plan the next step forward. This was also often the way Jesus interacted with those who came to him with questions.

THE QUESTION IN CONTEXT

In this case, Jesus is addressing his question to a group of John's disciples. They have come from visiting John, who was in prison. Their mission was to confront Jesus with a bold question, which John had sent them to ask. The question on John's mind was "Are you the one who is to come, or are we to look for another?"

For us to appreciate Jesus' answer, we must first take the time to remember the one who is asking the question. The question does not come from a curious Pharisee, an enquiring lawyer, or a would-be disciple. The question comes from John, the same John who baptized Jesus and introduced him to the world.

In this chapter not only will we learn from the question that Jesus asked, but also we will learn from John's question. John

> **When a leader has a clear mental picture of the future and the future fails to develop according to that picture, doubts can arise.**

was in prison (Luke 3:20) and he was beginning to raise questions based on what he had heard of Jesus' ministry. It is reasonable to think that the loneliness of a prison cell would give way to all manner of questions. It is also reasonable to assume that different persons take vastly different approaches to leadership. Could it be that John was second-guessing his identification of Jesus as the Messiah? Might the one who so boldly proclaimed, "Look, the Lamb of God, who takes away the sins of the world" (John 1:29), have lost his confidence in Jesus? It certainly appears that way. But why?

When a leader has a clear mental picture of the future (what's often referred to as "vision") and the future fails to develop according to that picture, doubts can arise. The leader begins to wonder, "Was I wrong? Did I misread or misunderstand the situation?"

Couple this second-guessing with a personal crisis or life stress (such as imprisonment), and those doubts begin to multiply. This is why self-care as a leader is so critical. It's harder to be steady, more difficult to be positive, when in the midst of a personal crisis. And the doubt and disappointment of a leader can quickly spread to the group. It is probable that this happened with John and his disciples. His question may well have become their question by the time they located Jesus and asked, "Are you the one who is to come, or are we to wait for another?"

What do we know about John and his ministry? Terms such as "maverick," "eccentric," and "prophet" may come to mind. John was a man of action. He confronted the hypocrisy and corruption of religion in his day and called persons to repentance. His was an unorthodox approach, from his clothing to his location to his message. He announced that the kingdom of heaven was at hand (Matthew 3:2).

It's likely that John, and his disciples, expected that kingdom to be of this earth. This would have meant a military overthrowing of Rome's hold on power. They yearned for a restoration of Israel as a sovereign nation and the promised Messiah as its king.

When Jesus also came preaching a kingdom of God at hand, John must have been hopeful and expectant. But when the kingdom failed to develop according to John's predetermined timeline and picture, doubts emerged.

IMPLICATIONS FOR LIFE AND LEADERSHIP

But let's not be too hard on John. Take a moment to consider when last you experienced a crisis that shook your life at its foundation. Perhaps it was the death of a loved one, a personal health crisis, or an unexpected turn of events related to a group to which you belong. Maybe it was just the accumulation of many things. How did that crisis impact your thinking? How did it affect your faith? Your prayer life? Your relationship with God? How did it change your leadership?

In the summer of 2014 Dan found himself in one of those lonely places. The church had just celebrated a significant achievement. The congregation had responded to a challenge from the pastor and various leadership teams to participate in a one-day giving challenge to support and address several ministry projects. The response was remarkable because in one day the congregation had raised gifts equivalent to 40 percent of their annual budget, for ministry outside that budget. We were even able to pay off our remaining mortgage with a "We're debt-free!" scream, à la Dave Ramsey![2]

In the days that followed many accolades and congratulations came Pastor Dan's way, affirming his leadership and the strong response of the congregation. It was a victory, the clear evidence of God's people working together. But, something wasn't right. Something wasn't right with the leader.

As the good feelings and warm regard for what had been accomplished gave way to a considerable amount of work to bring funded projects into reality, passions and opinions surfaced among congregants and anxiety rose in the congregational system. It may well be that the only thing more challenging for a church than not having enough money is having money! As the number of concerns and opinions multiplied regarding the management and expenditure of these funds, the worries, complaints, criticisms, and needs of congregants to express themselves usually found voice at the pastor's door.

But that was only one part of the equation. Dan had realized two significant familial losses in that same year. His dad passed away after a protracted decline from Parkinson's disease, and nine months later a sister died from brain cancer. Her death had come nearly ten years after their oldest sister had succumbed to a similar fight.

Personal crises in the lives of leaders often reframe how they look at leadership.

The accumulation of these things, on top of leading an active congregation and the challenges presented by their present opportunities, proved overwhelming, and the pastor realized that he needed help. His self-diagnosis was depression. When he described his feelings to a pastoral counselor who specializes in clergy issues, she said, "You've just described the classic symptoms of burnout."

When we experience a personal crisis like this, which takes us from the mountaintop of inspiration to the valley of despair, we often question God with our "whys." Our confidence in faith and in ourselves can be shaken. Our vision becomes limited to the proximity of our immediate situation in a self-centered and sometimes self-survival kind of way. In our self-talk we may even become convinced that we deserve better (or at least we don't deserve this) and find that resentment has taken up residence in our person.

In such times questions have a way of forming: "Is this what I signed on for?" "Has God forgotten me?" "Are you the One, or should I look for another?"

This phenomenon is seen over and over again in church leadership today. Clergy often journey through emotional highs and lows with congregants and congregations as part of ministry. Many arrive at a new pastorate with a vision of the future that is positive and hopeful. But they enter a story that has been a long time in development. Challenges come. Even healthy churches today face frustrating cultural and societal trends in attendance and giving that create tight budgets and plateaus or declines in participation. Any amount of organizational dysfunction only exponentially magnifies the leadership stresses. Add to this a leader's personal crisis—such as managing debt, a rocky marriage, family health emergency, or accumulated grief—and you've created a recipe that is ripe for second thoughts.

The reality of the work and struggle of leadership often does not add up to what the new pastor or seminary graduate imagined in his or her ideal picture. This may, in part, explain why many clergy exit pastoral ministry within the first five years. It also often triggers premature pastoral moves and creates trends in short-term pastorates.

Congregational lay leaders are not immune from such challenges either. Many of them are leaders in their vocational roles through the workweek, facing professional leadership challenges and juggling personal lives and situations. Persons who experience leadership struggles and burdens in their vocational life are less likely to want to engage in those same struggles in the church, making it difficult to recruit and retain volunteer leaders. As the church becomes filled with the brokenness of the world in which it ministers, the messiness of leading is magnified and questions arise.

BACK TO THE QUESTION IN CONTEXT

Notice in the Scripture passage that Jesus, in his reply, redirected John's question: "Go and tell John what you have seen and heard" (v. 22). Rather than offer a simple yes-or-no response, Jesus invited reflection on John's part, providing a list of actions for which Jesus had been responsible: the blind see, the lame walk, those with leprosy are cured, the dead are raised, and good news is preached to the poor. All of it was consistent with the message Jesus first preached (Luke 4:16-21). Jesus was active in bringing about the things of the kingdom, just not in the way John imagined.

A simple "yes" would likely have been followed by other questions. Instead, Jesus provided further food for thought by engaging John and his disciples in reflection. Jesus repeated three times to them, "What then did you go out to see?" Jesus was engaging John's disciples in a process of reflection that would lead them to their own answer. He wanted them to examine their own motivations for why they were attracted to John's message. Jesus was a master at drawing the circle wider and inviting individuals to grapple with the issues. This in itself is a leadership technique.

> Jesus was a master at drawing the circle wider and inviting individuals to grapple with the issues.

By asking the group to reflect, a leader—Jesus in this case—
gives them an opportunity to own the task or challenge for
themselves. What, in fact, should the kingdom of God look
like? How might it be introduced? Do we recognize it in our
midst? Is this it?

In a way, Jesus' response challenged John and the others
to stop limiting their definition of God's activity to their preconceived notions, or their personal experiences, and to look
and take heart at what was happening in the world. Persons
were becoming whole. God was being revealed in a loving
way. Look beyond the prison cell, the crisis, the challenge,
and see what God is about.

MORE IMPLICATIONS FOR
LIFE AND LEADERSHIP

Yes, congregational life today is different than it was in previous decades. There is no doubt that we can point to trends
and patterns that are of concern and require adaptive thinking
and approaches in leadership. But a beginning place is to look
up and see that, despite the challenges, God is still at work in
people's lives. God's kingdom is still in our midst—at hand.

Verses 23-30 of this text provide something of a postscript
to Jesus' encounter with John's question. As John's disciples
took their leave, Jesus intentionally turned the conversation
that he was having with the crowd to John. He began with
a blessing (v. 23): "Blessed is anyone who takes no offense
at me." That blessing also sounds like a warning, doesn't it?

But next we see the humility of Jesus as a leader. It is further accentuated in the following verses where he heaped
praise on John. The questions he asked, "What then did you
go out to see?" pointed out the obvious differences between
his own and John's leadership style. They also allowed him
opportunity to show respect for John and his ministry. Jesus had demonstrated that God uses different leaders with
differing styles for common purpose. Perhaps he was asking

the crowd to acknowledge the legitimacy of each leader and their message about God's kingdom, despite their differences in approach.

Congregational life today is different . . . but God's kingdom is still in our midst.

When you look at chapters of leadership across the landscape of one long-established congregation, you can sometimes, not always, but sometimes, see how the same church has greatly benefited in those differing chapters from leaders who, like John and Jesus, exhibited different styles but pointed to the same goals and the same God. That is something to be celebrated and acknowledged, the gift of a group of people who allow a leader to be whom he or she is gifted and called to be, and not force that leader into the mold of a predecessor.

Jesus' closing words at the end of verse 28 pulled back from praise and offered invitation: "yet the least in the kingdom of God is greater than he." It was the invitation to humility and the invitation to service. It's a phrase that indicates that there is room for each one of us in the journey of discipleship that Jesus has introduced. It's a reminder that it is God's kingdom that is important, and that we, all of us, are blessed to proclaim and bear witness to it.

Questions for Group Discussion or Personal Reflection

Please read Luke 7:18-30.

1. Think of a time when you used a question to respond to a question. What was the occasion? What was the outcome?
2. When have you made a significant life choice and then had second thoughts about it being the right choice? What was the choice? How did it work out?
3. What were the circumstances influencing John asking this question and Jesus responding with a question? In what ways are they comparable to those circumstances

surrounding your choice in the illustration in question 2 above?

4. If you were a disciple of John, how would your opinion of John have been influenced by him raising this question? When have you begun to doubt a leader because he or she questioned his or her own vision?

5. In what ways have you limited God to your own preconceived notions and then discovered that God is far greater than your limitations?

6. What do you learn from this account that will be a source of encouragement and strength when you face your next crisis?

Notes

1. Peter Scazzero, *The Emotionally Healthy Church: A Strategy for Discipleship That Actually Changes Lives* (Grand Rapids: Zondervan, 2003), 20.

2. Dave Ramsey is a best-selling author and a popular national talk-radio host on personal finance. Dave Ramsey, *Total Money Makeover: A Proven Plan for Financial Fitness* (Nashville: Thomas Nelson, 2013).

Appendix A

See how many of the following Bible questions you are familiar with. Identify who asked the question, where it is asked, to whom it is addressed, and where in the Bible it is found.

QUESTIONS				
Bible Question	Asked by Whom?	Where?	Addressed to Whom?	Scripture
Where are you?				
Who told you that you are naked?				
What are you doing here?				
Who touched me?				
Where were you when I laid the foundations of the earth?				
Whom shall I send, and who will go for us?				
Who is my neighbor?				
Why do you look for the living among the dead?				
If God is for us, who can be against us?				

	ANSWERS			
Bible Question	Asked by Whom?	Where?	Addressed to Whom?	Scripture
Where are you?	God	The garden of Eden	Adam and Eve	Genesis 3:9
Who told you that you are naked?	God	The garden of Eden	Adam and Eve	Genesis 3:11
What are you doing here?	God	A mountain cave	Elijah	1 Kings 19:9
Who touched me?	Jesus	On the road to Jairus's house	A crowd (woman with the hemorrhage)	Luke 8:45
Where were you when I laid the foundations of the earth?	God	Job's home	Job	Job 38:4
Whom shall I send, and who will go for us?	God	The Jerusalem temple	The prophet Isaiah	Isaiah 6:8
Who is my neighbor?	Young man	Along the road	Jesus	Luke 10:29
Why do you look for the living among the dead?	Angel	The garden tomb	Some women disciples	Luke 24:5
If God is for us, who can be against us?	Paul	Corinth or Cenchreae	Christians in the Roman Church	Romans 8:31

Appendix B

Many organizations, including the church, are facing challenges of discontinuous change today. Adaptive leaders will realize the importance of asking questions. **Leadership coaching** through the use of powerful questions can unlock a leader and group from what was previously considered a stuck situation into forward movement. Here are some examples of leadership coaching questions. Notice how they start very broad and gradually narrow in focus to help the person or group toward movement.

COACHING QUESTIONS

- How can I be most useful to you in this (coaching) conversation?
- What (in your work, relationship, life) feels most urgent right now?
- What's the best use of our time together? (Where do you want to focus?)
- What have you done thus far?
- What are you thinking about as a next step?
- What other options are you considering?
- What are some obstacles you might face?
- What consequences might there be?
- What resources will you need? Where do you think you can you find them?
- Who might you talk to about this? Where else could you turn?
- What will you do first? When?

Notice how, as the questions progress, they help the person narrow a focus and deal with obstacles. It's all about forward movement:

- Establishing focus
- Discovering possibilities
- Planning the action
- Removing barriers
- Recapping the plan

Where are you currently experiencing a feeling of being "stuck"? What challenge are you facing for which your prior experience and knowledge are not proving sufficient? Consider applying some of the above questions to that situation and see if you uncover some new possibilities.

What questions did you choose? Why? What was the outcome?

Appendix C

The following are additional questions that may be helpful for individuals to ponder before reading each of the chapters, and in preparation for small group discussion. The suggested process for approaching this study is:
1. Read the Scripture assigned to the chapter.
2. Ponder and reflect on the questions listed here related to that chapter.
3. Read the chapter and respond to the questions at the end of each chapter.

Introduction
1. How does the action of "questioning" relate back to the meaning of its root word, "quest"?
2. What is significant about the first recorded question in the Gospels that Jesus asked? What do you think their dialogue meant to the original audience? What does it mean to you?
3. What are some of the questions you can recall Jesus asking?
4. Why do you think Jesus made such use of questions when he taught and engaged with others?

Chapter 1: "Do You Want to Get Well?" (John 5:1-18)
1. What do we know about this pool of Beth-zatha, or as some translations have it, Bethsaida? What seems to be significant about the setting for this miracle? Why?
2. Why do you think Jesus focused his attention of this particular man out of all the others gathered by the

pool? What does Jesus' focus on this man tell us about Jesus himself?

3. What obstacles did this man face? How might these obstacles have accumulated in his life and in his thinking?

4. Why does Jesus engage the man in conversation? Why not just heal him and fix the situation?

5. Why do you think the Jewish authorities were so disturbed? What might be disturbing to us today about Jesus' intervention in our lives?

Chapter 2: "Who Touched My Clothes?" (Mark 5:21-43)

1. How does the back story, what has transpired in Mark 5:1-20, help you appreciate what Jesus may have felt as he arrives on shore in verse 21?

2. How would you describe the emotional state of the synagogue ruler who seeks Jesus' help? What about the emotional state of the woman with the hemorrhage?

3. What words would you use to describe Jesus' response to the interruptions and requests made in this passage?

Chapter 3: "What Do You Want Me to Do for You?" (Mark 10:32-52)

1. Where does this story take place? What do you know about this location?

2. Who are the principal characters? What is Jesus trying to teach them?

3. How do these characters respond differently to the same question from Jesus?

4. What is the reason for the crowd? Who are they? Where are they going?

5. What is Bartimaeus's daily routine? What is his request? How is his response received by the crowd?

6. What did Jesus do? What question did he ask? What command did he give? What action did he take?

7. How did Bartimaeus respond?

Chapter 4: "Do You Also Wish to Go Away?" (John 6:51-71)

1. How would those who were listening have found the language used by Jesus regarding "eating flesh" and "drinking blood"?
   a. familiar and normal
   b. abhorrent
   c. gross
   d. unfamiliar and strange
2. What did Jesus mean when he said, "Eat my flesh"?
3. What did Jesus mean when he said, "Drink my blood"?
4. How did the followers respond to such talk?
   a. They found it offensive.
   b. They found it difficult to listen to.
   c. Jesus was stepping on their toes.
   d. They looked for a different leader.
5. What else might we be offended by when examining the life of Jesus?
6. What question did Jesus ask the disciples who were also offended?
7. What are some possible sayings and expectations of Jesus that may offend people today?

Chapter 5: "Are You Still Sleeping and Resting?" (Matthew 26:36-56)

1. What do you know about Gethsemane?
2. How do you explain the disciples' sleeping at that important time?
3. How do we begin to understand Judas's role in these events? Explain your opinion.
   a. He was chosen to fulfill prophecy.
   b. He didn't want his sacred traditions destroyed.
   c. He believed the kingdom was coming.
   d. He was greedy.
   e. Other.

4. In the confrontation in the garden, who appeared to be in charge?

Chapter 6: "Do You Believe This?" (John 11:1-53)

1. What kind of relationships did Jesus appear to have with the family (Martha, Mary, and Lazarus) who lived in Bethany?
2. What type of response would you have expected from Jesus when given news of Lazarus's illness? How did he respond differently from what you would expect?
3. What other groups were present at Bethany (Martha and Mary's home)? How did they contribute to the biblical story?

Chapter 7: "Do You Love Me More Than These?" (John 21:1-17)

1. Some people have advised, "Don't do anything you can't live with for the rest of your life." How would you characterize this advice? Why?
   a. good
   b. possible
   c. impossible
   d. realistic
   e. discouraging
2. Look up these experiences of Peter that may have been difficult for him to live with for the rest of his life: (a) Matthew 16:21-23; (b) John 13:3-11; (c) John 13:36-38; (d) John 18:10-11; (e) John 18:17-18, 25-27; (f) Luke 24:8-12.
3. What does the text tell us the disciples had witnessed regarding the resurrection of Jesus?
4. How do you imagine professional fishers would normally respond to someone on the shore telling them where to catch fish?
5. Where does Peter's renewal actually start in this text?

6. How does Jesus' conversation with Peter reveal Jesus' evaluation of Peter's need?

Chapter 8: "What Then Did You Go Out to See?" (Luke 7:18-30)

1. Who are the individuals in this text? What are we told about them? (See also Luke 3:19-20; Acts 18:24–19:4.)
2. What "things" did John's disciples report to him?
3. What is so startling about their inquiry on behalf of John? Why?
4. What could have happened to change John's mind from certainty to doubt?
5. How might John's personal circumstances have contributed to this doubt?
6. What happens in groups where the leader begins to express doubts?
7. Why did Jesus not answer with a simple "yes"? How does Jesus' question to them prepare them to return to John with an answer?
8. What was the postscript Jesus gave to the messengers to give to John? What did it mean?
9. What tribute did Jesus pay to John? How did Jesus use questions to engage his audience in thinking about John and John's role?
10. How different was Jesus' style of leadership compared to John's?
11. Name two leaders in your own life's journey who had very different styles but who were effective leaders. How did their styles differ? What lessons did you learn from each of them?

About the Authors

Daniel M. Cash, DMin

Dan Cash currently serves as senior pastor of the First Baptist Church of Columbus, Indiana. With more than twenty-five years in pastoral and regional ministry, Dan completed his Doctor of Ministry in 2008 with a dissertation titled "Understanding the Pastoral Role in Leading Change." He is married to Lori, and together they are parents of three young adult children.

William H. Griffith, DMin

Bill Griffith is a retired American Baptist pastor and hospice chaplain who has written three books on the topics of death and grief. Two books were published by Judson Press: *Confronting Death* and *More Than a Parting Prayer: Lessons in Care-Giving for the Dying*. He lives in Columbus, Indiana, with his wife, Lois, and they are members of the First Baptist Church, where he was once senior pastor.

In recent years Bill and Dan have collaborated in leading a weekly men's small group. This book was developed from material first written and shared in that ministry.